GREAT PLANTS
50
For TENNESSEE GARDENS

SHRUBS
for
TENNESSEE

SHRUBS *for* TENNESSEE

Judy Lowe

COOL
SPRINGS
PRESS

Nashville, Tennessee
A Division of Thomas Nelson, Inc.
www.ThomasNelson.com

Published by Cool Springs Press, a Division of Thomas Nelson, Inc., P.O. Box 141000, Nashville, Tennessee, 37214.

First printing 2004
Printed in the United States of America
10 9 8 7 6 5 4 3 2 1

Managing Editor: Mary Morgan
Horticulture Editor: Michael Wenzel, Atlanta Botanical Garden
Copyeditor: Michelle Adkerson
Designer: Bill Kersey, Kersey Graphics
Production Artist: S.E. Anderson

On the cover: Hydrangea, photographed by Thomas Eltzroth

We gratefully acknowledge the contributions of the following authors who have granted their permission to use selected entries:

Mountain Laurel (pg. 72)—Liz Ball; Miss Kim Lilac (pg. 70)—Tim Boland, Laura Coit, and Marty Hair; Juniper (pg. 58) and Winter Daphne (pg. 108)—Walter Reeves and Erica Glasener; Hybrid Tea Rose (pg. 54), Juniper (pg. 58), Landscape Rose (pg. 62), Miniature Rose (pg. 68), Oakleaf Hydrangea (pg. 76), Old Garden Rose (pg. 78); Pieris (pg. 82), and Pyracantha (pg. 86)—Toby Bost; Bluebeard (pg. 16), Glossy Abelia (pg. 52), Hybrid Tea Rose (pg. 54), Mountain Laurel (pg. 72), Oregon Grape Holly (pg. 80), Purple Japanese Barberry (pg. 84), Pyracantha (pg. 86), and Weigela (pg. 104)—Andre Viette and Jacqueline Heriteau

Visit the Thomas Nelson website at www.ThomasNelson.com

Table *of* Contents

How To Use This Book

Each entry in this guide provides you with information about a plant's particular characteristics, habits, and basic requirements for active growth as well as my personal experience and knowledge of the plant. I include the information you need to help you realize each plant's potential. Only when a plant performs at its best can one appreciate it fully. You will find such pertinent information as mature height and spread, bloom period and colors (if any), sun and soil preferences, water requirements, fertilizing needs, pruning and care, and pest information.

Sun Preferences

Symbols represent the range of sunlight suitable for each plant. Some plants can be grown in more than one range of sun, so you will sometimes see more than one sun symbol.

Full Sun   **Part Sun/Shade**   **Full Shade**

Additional Benefits

Many plants offer benefits that further enhance their appeal. The following symbols indicate some of the more important additional benefits:

 Attracts Butterflies

 Attracts Hummingbirds

 Produces Edible Fruit

 Has Fragrance

 Produces Food for Birds and Wildlife

 Drought Resistant

 Suitable for Cut Flowers or Arrangements

 Long Bloom Period

 Native Plant

 Supports Bees

 Good Fall Color

 Provides Shelter for Birds

Complementary Plants

For many of the entries, I provide landscape design ideas as well as suggestions for companion plants to help you achieve striking and personal gardening results from your garden. This is where I find the most enjoyment from gardening.

Recommended Selections

This section describes specific cultivars or varieties that I have found particularly noteworthy. Give them a try.

50 Great Shrubs *for* Tennessee

Shrubs are the second most important plants in your yard—only trees are more important. But you'll have more shrubs than trees, and they will likely define your yard in a way no other plant can. Banks of red, pink, and white azaleas can transform your landscape into a springtime paradise. Shrubs such as camellia and witchhazel flower in the cold winter months when the sight of blossoms is a rare and especially welcome treat. Hedges separate your land from your neighbor's, and shrubs planted as a screen ensure privacy or block an unsightly view.

Something for Everyone

Shrubs are a most versatile group of plants. They come in forms ranging from pyramidal to rounded to columnar and with varied textures that can be mixed and matched for a pleasing effect. Shrubs with small leaves look neat and fit nicely in confined spaces. Shrubs with larger leaves are bolder looking and ideal for larger areas, especially where they'll be seen from a distance.

Shrubs can be colorful, too—and not just those that flower. If you like a large splash of color, look for shrubs with gold, purple, or red foliage or those with variegated leaves. But don't overdo it—for the best results, use these colorful shrubs as accents in a sea of green.

Shrubs may be evergreen—either broadleafed, such as boxwood, or needled, such as false cypress. Or they may be deciduous and lose their leaves in fall. Usually, evergreens are placed

Nandina

in the most prominent spots for year-round effect and deciduous shrubs fade into the background except when they're flowering.

Plan Ahead

Whether you're happy with your shrub selection or not depends more than anything else on how well you match its mature size to the spot where you want to put it. When you're planting a 1-gallon azalea, it's hard to imagine that someday it will be 4 feet tall and at least as wide—but it probably will. So if you plant a half-dozen of them about a foot apart, in a few years, you'll find yourself digging up every other one. And a few years after that, you'll have to do the same thing again. It's much easier to plant a small shrub than to dig up a large one and move it. If those newly planted shrubs look skimpy, fill in between them with annuals or perennials until the shrubs reach their mature sizes.

Planting ABCs

Before you buy any shrub, always check the root system to make sure it's in good shape. Don't buy a shrub that's rootbound—one whose roots wind round and round the ball of soil. It's difficult to get such a plant to grow well again.

When you're ready to plant, dig a hole twice as wide as the rootball and about the same depth. This is to prevent the newly planted shrub from sinking into the hole and ending up lower than it was in its container, which can lead to root rot.

Oakleaf Hydrangea

Witchhazel

Mix the soil from the hole with fine bark, compost, or other organic matter. Carefully remove the well-watered shrub from its pot, and place it on firm soil at the bottom of the hole. Replace the amended soil firmly around the shrub's roots, making a shallow saucer or indented circle around the shrub on top of the soil—this is to hold water. Water slowly and thoroughly, and continue watering regularly if rainfall totals less than an inch a week. Spread mulch around the shrub to hold moisture in the soil and to keep down weeds. Never fertilize a shrub at planting time— wait until the next spring.

With all this in mind, you're ready to browse through the following pages to find the shrubs that will work best for you. Whether you're looking for flowers, berries, three or four seasons of interest, plants to attract birds and other small wildlife, a screen or hedge, or just something that's plain good looking in your yard, you're sure to find the perfect choice.

Aucuba

Aucuba japonica

An Old-Fashioned Favorite with Variegated Foliage to Brighten the Shade

Aucuba went through a period when it was considered hopelessly old-fashioned and much overplanted. That didn't deter me. To my mind, a broadleafed evergreen that brightens shady corners with gold and green variegated leaves is a keeper. Now aucuba has been restored to horticultural good graces and is easy to find in nurseries. I'm trying to see how many different cultivars I can find.

Top Reasons to Plant

○ Variegated gold and green foliage
○ Thrives in shade
○ Foliage effective year-round
○ Red berries in fall and winter
○ Few pests or diseases

Useful Hint

Aucuba may not be suitable for the coldest parts of Tennessee, but if you like its looks, it's worth taking a chance on growing it.

Bloom Color
Maroon to purple

Bloom Period
Early spring

Height/Width
6 to 15 feet x 5 to 10 feet

Planting Location
- Moist, well-drained soil with plenty of organic matter
- Shade or mostly shade year-round

Planting
- Plant in spring for best effect, but container-grown plants may be set out from May until the end of August if kept well watered.
- Dig the hole twice as wide as the rootball and about the same depth.
- Add compost or finely shredded bark to the soil removed from the hole.
- Place the shrub in the hole, half-fill the hole with soil mixture, and water with transplanting solution.
- Fill the hole with soil mixture.
- Water well.
- Mulch with pine straw or fine bark.

Watering
- Adequate moisture is a must.
- Keep the soil slightly damp when the plant is young.
- After the shrub becomes established, water deeply when weekly rainfall doesn't total an inch.

Easy Tip
To ensure a good crop of berries, plant both a male and a female cultivar.

Fertilizing
- At the end of April, if desired, spread a slow-release shrub fertilizer around the plant's base.

Suggestions for Vigorous Growth
- Prune to keep shape neat and rounded, using hand pruners to cut stems back to just above a bud.

Pest Control
- Few insects or disease problems bother this shrub.

Complementary Plants
- Use for foundation plantings on the north side of the house or beneath tall pines.
- Group with other shade-loving shrubs in a woodland bed.

Recommended Selections
- 'Variegata' is one of the hardiest cultivars.
- 'Nana' grows 3 to 5 feet tall and has abundant berries.

Beautyberry

Callicarpa species and hybrids

A Stunner with Lavender-Purple Berries in Fall

I like to have a mixture of plants in my yard—some that are familiar old friends and others that are so different and such standouts they make people stop and ask, "What in the world is that?" Although easy to grow, beautyberry is in the latter group. Most of the year, this deciduous shrub doesn't call attention to itself. But in late summer and fall, when it's covered with lavender to purple berries, wow! And they last quite a long time, often into winter.

Top Reasons to Plant

O Showy berries late summer and fall
O Attracts butterflies
O Few insects and diseases
O Naturalizes well
O Likes average soil

Useful Hint

While beautyberry grows well in partial shade, it produces a lot more berries in full sun.

Bloom Color
Pink or lavender followed by purplish or white fruits

Bloom Period
Summer, with berries in fall

Height/Width
3 to 10 feet x 4 to 8 feet

Planting Location
• Average soil, preferably not rich
• Sun to partial sun—full sun is best for berry production

Planting
• Plant anytime from spring till fall.
• Dig the hole twice as wide as the rootball and about the same depth.
• Add compost or finely shredded bark to the soil removed from the hole.
• Place the shrub in the hole, half-fill the hole with soil mixture, and water with transplanting solution.
• Fill the hole with soil mixture.
• Mulch to keep down weeds.

Watering
• Ample water is needed for this shrub to produce plentiful fruits.
• Soak weekly if summer rainfall is deficient.

Fertilizing
• Do not fertilize—doing so causes too much stem growth at the expense of berries.

Suggestions for Vigorous Growth
• Cut out dead stems in late winter or early spring.

Easy Tip

If the top of the beautyberry plant is killed in a severe winter, it will grow back from the roots.

• Prune Japanese beautyberry (*Callicarpa japonica*) back to 2 feet tall to encourage new growth with lots of flowers and berries.
• Any overgrown beautyberry may be cut back to 1 foot tall in early spring and allowed to regrow.

Pest Control
• No serious insects or diseases trouble beautyberry.

Complementary Plants
• Naturalize American beautyberry under tall pine trees that have been limbed up.
• All beautyberries are stunning in fall when massed in groups.

Recommended Selections
• Purple beautyberry (*Callicarpa dichotoma*) is very graceful and colorful.
• 'Early Amethyst' is a cultivar reaching about 4 feet by 4 feet.
• American beautyberry (*Callicarpa americana*) naturalizes well.

Bluebeard

Caryopteris × clandonensis

An Easy Shrub with Delightful Blue Flowers in Midsummer

Bluebeard, sometimes called blue spirea, is a small, easy deciduous shrub that in August produces spikes of airy flowers in delightful shades of blue. The long arching branches are covered in silvery leaves, and the entire plant is delicately aromatic. It grows quickly and develops an open, airy shape that is very appealing in flower borders and makes an attractive edging along walks and paths. It blooms on new wood in midsummer or later when most other flowering shrubs are done.

Top Reasons to Plant

- Beautiful blue flowers in late summer
- Small scale
- Easy to grow
- Good cut flower
- Good dried flower
- Attracts butterflies and hummingbirds
- Few pests and diseases

Useful Hint

To improve bloom, cut bluebeard back severely in late winter or early spring.

Bloom Color
Shades of blue

Bloom Period
Midsummer to late summer

Height/Width
2 to 3 feet x 3 to 4 feet

Planting Location
• Well-drained, loose, loamy soil
• Sun to light shade

Planting
• Plant in early spring or early fall.
• Dig the hole twice as wide as the rootball and about the same depth.
• Add compost or finely shredded bark to the soil removed from the hole.
• Place the shrub in the hole, half-fill the hole with soil mixture, and water with transplanting solution.
• Fill the hole with soil mixture.
• Mulch 3 inches deep starting 3 inches from the crown (where roots and stems meet).

Watering
• In the first year, water well every two weeks in spring and fall, and every week in summer—unless there's been an inch of rainfall per week.

Fertilizing
• Feed lightly with a slow-release, organic fertilizer in fall and again in late winter or early spring.

Easy Tip
Bluebeard foliage and flowers are both excellent in arrangements, fresh or dried.

Suggestions for Vigorous Growth
• Maintain mulch year-round.
• Since bluebeard blooms on new wood, improve flowering by cutting it back to 6 inches tall in later winter or very early spring.

Pest Control
• No serious pests or diseases trouble this shrub.

Complementary Plants
• Plant in perennial borders for an excellent effect.
• Outstanding in butterfly plantings.

Recommended Selections
• 'Longwood Blue' grows from $1^{1}/_{2}$ feet to 2 feet tall and has a heavy crop of deeper blue flowers against silvery foliage.
• 'Dark Knight' grows to 3 feet tall by 3 to 4 feet wide with very fragrant, dark purple-blue blooms that attract butterflies and hummingbirds.
• 'Blue Mist' is about the same size as 'Dark Knight'; it has fringed blue flowers.
• 'Worcester Gold' has blue flowers and bright-yellow to chartreuse foliage.

Boxwood

Buxus species and hybrids

A Treasured Southern Evergreen for a Handsome Shrub or Hedge

Across Tennessee, we've grown up with boxwoods. We've known them as useful foundation shrubs and as hedges. Visiting Colonial Williamsburg in Virginia and Andrew Jackson's home, the Hermitage, near Nashville, we've seen how enormous they can grow and how long they can live. Boxwoods are handsome, broad-leafed evergreens with many uses; they're especially nice to add winter interest to a perennial border.

Top Reasons to Plant

- Evergreen foliage
- Excellent hedge plant
- Gives winter form to perennial flower plantings
- Aromatic foliage
- Cut branches good for winter decorating

Useful Hint

If planting boxwoods in clay soil, amend the soil well with organic matter to improve drainage and to reduce the chance of root rot.

Height/Width
2 to 20 feet x 3 to 25 feet

Planting Location
- Moist, well-drained soil
- Sheltered from drying winds, if possible
- Sun or partial sun

Planting
- Plant in spring.
- Dig the hole twice as wide as the rootball and about the same depth.
- Add compost or finely shredded bark to the soil removed from the hole.
- Place the shrub in the hole, half-fill the hole with soil mixture, and water with transplanting solution.
- Fill the hole with soil mixture.
- Mulch well.

Watering
- Water deeply once a week when rainfall is lacking.

Fertilizing
- Feed each spring with a slow-release fertilizer for evergreen shrubs.

Suggestions for Vigorous Growth
- Maintain mulch year-round to protect shallow roots.
- Prune in early spring—damage may result from pruning after July.
- Use hand pruners rather than shears to improve resistance to snow and cold.

Easy Tip
If you want a rounded boxwood, save yourself a lot of work—read the label and choose a cultivar that grows that way naturally.

Pest Control
- Boxwood is subject to many insects and diseases.
- Off-color foliage in spring or summer usually indicates root rot caused by poor drainage.
- Nematodes may stunt roots.
- If root rot or nematodes are a problem, try moving the shrub elsewhere.

Complementary Plants
- Plant in formal or colonial-style gardens.
- Use as hedges.
- Use dwarf forms to edge herb or flower gardens.

Recommended Selections
- 'Green Mountain' is extremely hardy and carefree.
- *Buxus sempervirens* 'Elegantissima' has leaves edged in cream.

Buckeye

Aesculus species and hybrids

A Native Shrub with Showy Spring or Summer Flowers

Buckeye isn't just a tree—there are two native species that may be used as attractive flowering shrubs in Tennessee. One is bottlebrush buckeye (*Aesculus parviflora*), which has white flowers that look like the brushes you wash bottles with, only softer and larger—they're a foot long and 2 to 4 inches around. The other is red buckeye (*Aesculus pavia*), which in mid- to late spring has 6- to 8-inch red (or sometimes yellow) flower panicles popular with hummingbirds.

Top Reasons to Plant

- Beautiful blooms
- Attracts hummingbirds
- Few pests or diseases
- Thrives in shade
- Good fall color with bottlebrush buckeye

Useful Hint

Bottlebrush buckeye (*A. parviflora*) has leaves that turn yellow in fall.

Bloom Color
White (bottlebrush buckeye) or red (red buckeye)

Bloom Period
Bottlebrush buckeye blooms in mid-summer; red buckeye in spring

Height/Width
8 to 20 feet x 8 to 25 feet

Planting Location
- Moist, well-drained, acidic soil with organic matter added
- Full sun to full shade for bottlebrush buckeye; red buckeye prefers partial shade

Planting
- Choose a site where the shrubs have room to grow—they spread considerably and produce suckers, so don't crowd them.
- Plant in early spring before growth starts.
- Dig the hole twice as wide as the rootball and about the same depth.
- Add compost or finely shredded bark to the soil removed from the hole.
- Place the shrub in the hole, half-fill the hole with soil mixture, and water with transplanting solution.
- Fill the hole with soil mixture.
- Mulch.

Watering
- When the plant is young, water regularly to keep the soil moist.
- After that, water deeply any week when the rainfall measures less than an inch.

Easy Tip

Don't overcrowd these plants—they spread widely and produce suckers.

Fertilizing
- Fertilizer is not needed, but if growth isn't fast enough, use a slow-release shrub fertilizer at the end of March.

Suggestions for Vigorous Growth
- Prune in winter if needed to keep inbounds.
- Cut overgrown specimens back to ground level.
- Dig or pull up unwanted suckers anytime of the year.

Pest Control
- With shade and correct environmental conditions, pests and diseases shouldn't be a problem.

Complementary Plants
- These plants make nice specimen shrubs.
- Plant beneath limbed-up tall trees or in a shrub border.

Recommended Selections
- 'Rogers' has the largest flowers I've seen on a bottlebrush buckeye and usually blooms a couple of weeks later than the native species.

Burning Bush

Euonymus alatus

A Shrub That Turns Fire-Engine Red, and Then Some, in Fall

Fluorescent-red, fire-engine-red, brilliant-scarlet—attempts to describe the fall color of burning bush simply don't do it justice. This deciduous shrub is one of the most reliable plants for spectacular fall foliage. While other shrubs may look fabulous in some years, and okay in others, burning bush always comes through. Although a true star in autumn, it's modest in its requirements, being adaptable to almost any situation except wet soil and extreme drought.

Top Reasons to Plant

- Striking fall color
- Adaptable to varying soils
- Few pests and diseases
- Tolerates range of light conditions
- Good screen or hedge plant

Useful Hint

You can remove the lower limbs of burning bush and grow it as a small tree.

Bloom Color
Insignificant yellowish flowers

Bloom Period
Late spring

Height/Width
6 to 20 feet x 10 to 20 feet

Planting Location
- Any average soil that doesn't stay wet
- Sun or partial sun for best color, but tolerates shade

Planting
- Plant in early spring.
- Dig the hole twice as wide as the rootball and about the same depth.
- Add compost or finely shredded bark to the soil removed from the hole.
- Place the shrub in the hole, half-fill the hole with soil mixture, and water with transplanting solution.
- Fill the hole with soil mixture.
- Mulch with several inches of pine straw or fine pine bark.

Watering
- Regular watering is best if rainfall is below normal, but this shrub can tolerate occasional dryness.

Fertilizing
- This shrub grows slowly, so apply slow-release fertilizer in early spring each year before the plant leafs out.

Easy Tip

Burning bush has absolutely reliable, stunning fall color, every year.

Suggestions for Vigorous Growth
- Maintain mulch so soil doesn't dry out.
- Little pruning is required, but you may shear the plant regularly if it's grown as a hedge.

Pest Control
- Few serious disease or insect problems trouble this shrub.

Complementary Plants
- Place in front of evergreens where its glowing fall color is more noticeable.
- This shrub makes a good, colorful screening plant.

Recommended Selections
- 'Compactus' isn't quite as small as its name makes it sound—about 10 feet high, though it grows slowly—but it has a nice shape and outstanding fall leaf color.
- 'Rudy Haag' is about half as tall as 'Compactus', making it great for small spaces, and its fall foliage tends to be more rosy than screaming-red.

Buttercup Winterhazel
Corylopsis pauciflora

A Dainty Beauty with Lovely, Fragrant Yellow Blooms in Early Spring

In spring, the bare spreading branches of the buttercup winterhazel are covered with fragrant, primrose-yellow flowers dangling in short clusters of two or three. Blooming about the same time as forsythia, it is more delicate and elegant in appearance and in size, making it an excellent choice for small yards. Buttercup winterhazel has an attractive growing habit, pretty leaves, and straw-yellow fall foliage.

Top Reasons to Plant

- Dangling, pastel-yellow blooms
- Fragrant flowers
- Refined, graceful form
- Nice fall color
- Disease and pest resistant
- Tolerates moist soils
- Fits well into smaller gardens

Useful Hint

Buttercup winterhazel is a wonderful choice for yellow flowers in early spring in small gardens.

Bloom Color
Primrose-yellow

Bloom Period
Late winter to early spring

Height/Width
4 to 6 feet x 4 to 6 feet

Planting Location
- Well-drained, moist, acidic soil with lots of organic matter
- Sun to light shade

Planting
- Plant in spring.
- Dig the hole twice as wide as the rootball and about the same depth.
- Add compost or finely shredded bark to the soil removed from the hole.
- Place the shrub in the hole, half-fill the hole with soil mixture, and water with transplanting solution.
- Fill the hole with soil mixture.
- Mulch with several inches of pine straw or fine pine bark.

Watering
- Keep the soil moist while the tree is young.
- Once the tree becomes established, water deeply in weeks without an inch of rain.

Fertilizing
- No fertilizer is required.
- If desired, feed the plant in early spring with a slow-release fertilizer for acid-loving shrubs.

Easy Tip

The only serious enemy of this easy-to-grow, elegant beauty is drought.

Suggestions for Vigorous Growth
- Prune, if needed, after flowering.
- Shelter from winter winds and late frosts.

Pest Control
- No serious pests or diseases trouble this plant.

Complementary Plants
- Underplant with spring bulbs and early-flowering perennials such as the blue-flowering pulmonarias.
- Mass in a woodland setting for an excellent effect.
- Plant against a dark-evergreen background.

Recommended Selections
- Plant the species.

Butterfly Bush
Buddleja davidii

A Butterfly Magnet That People Like Too

If you've ever complained that fewer and fewer butterflies are visiting your yard—or that many are present one summer but not the next—you can quickly change the situation. Plant a butterfly bush. Its flowers are magnets to these winged jewels. The grayish foliage is attractive also, as is the shape of the shrub. Graceful 8- to 10-inch plumes of fragrant flowers are available in shades or purple and lavender, blue, magenta, pink, rose, and yellow to match any landscaping color scheme.

Top Reasons to Plant

- Beautiful plumes of flowers
- Wide range of colors
- Guaranteed to attract butterflies
- Graceful shape
- Long bloom period
- Fragrant flowers
- Few pests or diseases

Useful Hint

For best bloom, cut butterfly bush back to about a foot tall in early spring.

Bloom Color
Purple, blue, pink, yellow, or white

Bloom Period
Midsummer to frost

Height/Width
6 to 15 feet x 7 to 10 feet

Planting Location
- Best in fertile, moist, well-drained soil but tolerates just about any soil that's well drained
- Sun

Planting
- Plant in spring.
- Dig the hole twice as wide as the rootball and about the same depth.
- Add compost or finely shredded bark to the soil removed from the hole.
- Place the shrub in the hole, half-fill the hole with soil mixture, and water with transplanting solution.
- Fill the hole with soil mixture.
- Mulch with 2 to 3 inches of pine straw or fine pine bark.

Watering
- Butterfly bush survives some dryness but won't bloom well without ample moisture.
- Water deeply in weeks without at least an inch of rainfall.

Fertilizing
- Feed with slow-release fertilizer at the base of the shrub each spring when you cut it back.
- Make a light application of lime every other fall.

Easy Tip
Butterfly bush looks lovely cut for arrangements, but the flowers don't last long.

Suggestions for Vigorous Growth
- This plant blooms on new growth— be sure to cut the shrub back to about a foot tall in spring before leaves emerge.
- To prolong bloom, cut off flowers as they fade.

Pest Control
- Few insects or diseases bother this shrub.
- Avoid insecticides—they'll harm the butterflies.

Complementary Plants
- Mass several together for a beautiful show.
- Use as the centerpiece of a perennial border.

Recommended Selections
- 'Pink Delight' features large, fragrant, true-pink flowers.
- The stems of 'Peace' arch gracefully; its fragrant white blossoms have orange throats.

Camellia

Camellia species and hybrids

A Deep South Favorite Now Trustworthy in Tennessee

There's wonderful news on the camellia front—no longer are these beautiful flowering shrubs just for the warmest climates. A group of cold-hardy camellias, developed by Dr. William Ackerman of the National Arboretum, has extended their range throughout all of Tennessee. Now there's little reason for anyone to be without these exotic blooms in fall, winter, and early spring.

Top Reasons to Plant

○ Beautiful blossoms in cold weather
○ Attractive glossy, evergreen foliage
○ Usually few pests or diseases
○ Good cut flower
○ Tolerates cold depending on cultivar

Useful Hint

If you live in Memphis, Chattanooga, or an area with a similar climate, try some of the less hardy cultivars of *Camellia japonica* in a protected place. They're hardier than *Camellia sasanqua*, and even if the top growth is killed back by an unusually cold winter, they will generally grow back from the roots.

Bloom Color
Pink, white, red, or variegated

Bloom Period
Fall through spring

Height/Width
10 to 15 feet x 5 to 10 feet

Planting Location
• Moist, well-drained, acidic soil amended with lots of organic matter such as fine pine bark
• Partial shade—best placed on west side of the house or where evergreens block the morning sun in winter

Planting
• Plant in spring.
• Dig the hole twice as wide as the rootball and about the same depth.
• Add compost or finely shredded bark to the soil removed from the hole.
• Place the shrub in the hole, half-fill the hole with soil mixture, and water with transplanting solution.
• Fill the hole with soil mixture.
• Mulch with 2 to 3 inches of pine straw or fine pine bark.

Watering
• Water regularly when rainfall doesn't total an inch per week.
• This shrub's shallow root system cannot tolerate drought.

Fertilizing
• In March or April, feed with 1 pound of cottonseed meal per inch of trunk diameter spread around the plant's base.

Easy Tip
Although open camellia flowers may be damaged by temperatures below 32 degrees Fahrenheit, unopened buds won't be harmed.

• *Or* spray with water-soluble fertilizer for acid-loving plants after blooming ends.

Suggestions for Vigorous Growth
• To keep plant in shape, remove two or three leaves at the base of the bloom when you cut off faded flowers.
• Prune after flowering stops.
• To protect from severe cold snaps, cover with a blanket, mattress pad, or quilt—but not plastic.

Pest Control
• Potential problems are legion but generally don't occur.

Complementary Plants
• For an excellent effect, mass beneath tall pines with lower limbs 20 feet high.

Recommended Selections
• 'Polar Ice' is a cold-hardy variety with white flowers.
• 'Winter's Beauty', another cold-hardy type, features double pink blossoms.
• *Camellia japonica* 'Debutante' is an old pink favorite that's relatively hardy.

Carolina Allspice

Calycanthus floridus

An Incredibly Fragrant Bloomer with Good Fall Color

If you were to see Carolina allspice growing in my yard in August, you might wonder what was special about this deciduous shrub. But if you visited in April or May (sometimes even into July), you'd know the answer the minute you walked by it. The fragrance of the reddish maroon flowers has been described as similar to strawberries, pineapple, or banana, or all three. The scent reminds me of pineapple sage. However you describe the aroma, it's heavenly.

Top Reasons to Plant

○ Wonderful fragrance
○ Interesting spring blooms
○ No pests or diseases
○ Good fall color
○ Tolerates variety of soils
○ Thrives in sun to partial shade

Useful Hint

To ensure that the flowers are fragrant—seed-grown shrubs often have no scent—buy Carolina allspice when it's in bloom.

Bloom Color
Maroon

Bloom Period
Midspring into summer

Height/Width
6 to 10 feet x 6 to 12 feet

Planting Location
- Prefers moist, well-drained soil with organic matter, but tolerates average soil of any type
- Full sun to partial shade

Planting
- Plant in spring.
- Dig the hole twice as wide as the rootball and about the same depth.
- Add compost or finely shredded bark to the soil removed from the hole.
- Place the shrub in the hole, half-fill the hole with soil mixture, and water with transplanting solution.
- Fill the hole with soil mixture.
- Mulch with 2 to 3 inches of pine straw or fine pine bark.

Watering
- Keep soil moist around young shrubs.
- Once the shrub becomes established, water deeply if there hasn't been an inch total of rainfall during the week.

Fertilizing
- Feed with slow-release shrub fertilizer in March or April, following label directions.

Easy Tip
Carolina allspice adapts to everything from full sun to partial shade—if you don't want it to grow too tall, give it full sun.

Suggestions for Vigorous Growth
- Little pruning is required.
- If needed, prune in very early spring or just after flowering—this shrub blooms on new growth, as well as last year's wood.

Pest Control
- No insects or diseases trouble this shrub.

Complementary Plants
- Plant in a border with other shrubs.
- Place near a walkway, patio, porch, garden bench, or chair to enjoy the fragrance.

Recommended Selections
- 'Michael Lindsey' has superb fragrance, good-looking foliage, and a nice yellow fall color.

31

Climbing Rose

Rosa species and hybrids

A Picturesque Fragrant Favorite That Doesn't Really Climb

The roses we call "climbers" put forth long canes that can be trained to cover an arch, an arbor, a trellis, a wall, or a fence, or to climb a tree. "Training" means being tied—roses don't climb on their own. The showiest climbers are ramblers with clusters of small blooms on flexible canes that rise annually from the base. Other climbers are tall shrubs with stiff canes bearing large flowers singly or in clusters. Either way, these beauties require some work on the part of the gardener.

Top Reasons to Plant

- Beautiful, showy flowers
- Fragrant blossoms on many varieties
- Extends landscape vertically
- Good cut flower
- Attracts butterflies

Useful Hint

Climbing roses trained to grow horizontally along fences tend to flower more than climbers growing straight up.

Bloom Color
White, yellow, pink, or red

Bloom Period
Depends on variety—some bloom spring till fall

Height/Width
6 to 20 feet x 3 to 6 feet

Planting Location
• Well-drained, fertile soil with lots of organic matter
• Sun, although climbers bloom well with their branches in sun and their roots in shade

Planting
• Plant bare-root roses in early spring and container roses in late spring.
• Dig the hole 24 inches wide and at least 18 inches deep.
• Mix soil with equal amounts of organic matter.
• For bare-root roses, build a cone of soil in the hole and drape roots over it. Remove container rose from pot and place in hole. Set rose so the bud union is 1 inch above ground level.
• Fill hole with amended soil.
• Water with transplanting solution.
• Mulch with pine straw or fine pine bark.

Watering
• In the plant's first year, water deeply every week, unless there has been an inch of rainfall.

Fertilizing
• Apply a slow-release rose fertilizer in early spring and monthly until early August.

Easy Tip
To reduce spraying chores, check into fertilizers with systemic insect controls incorporated into them.

Suggestions for Vigorous Growth
• Keep mulched year-round.
• Every year, remove one of the oldest canes, and save two or three of the new canes for next year—five or six heavy canes are all a climbing rose can support.
• Keep canes tied in with twine or the new Velcro™ plant ties to ensure they grow in the desired direction.

Pest Control
• Japanese beetles, blackspot, and powdery mildew are common.
• Check with your Extension Agent or garden center about controls that work well in your area.

Complementary Plants
• Underplant with catmint, lavender, or other bushy companions.

Recommended Selections
• For recurrent bloom all summer, 'Golden Showers' is yellow and fragrant, 'New Dawn' is fragrant blush-pink, and 'White Dawn' is fragrant white.
• Very fragrant climbers include 'Don Juan' (dark-red), 'Golden Artie' (gold), and 'Paul's Lemon Pillar' (yellow).

Crapemyrtle
Lagerstroemia species and hybrids

A Spectacular Summer Bloomer in Many Sizes and Colors

Plant breeders, particularly at the National Arboretum, have made huge strides forward with crapemyrtles. They're more cold hardy than before and come in many sizes, rather than just extra large. Another advance is that the newer cultivars aren't subject to mildew. They also bloom for a longer time than they did in the past. You can now have crapemyrtle in flower from June through September. And the newer types also have excellent fall color and beautiful bark.

Top Reasons to Plant

- Beautiful summer blooms
- Outstanding fall foliage
- Gorgeous winter bark
- Pest and disease resistant
- Wide range of colors
- Sizes ranging from tiny to huge
- Good cut flower

Useful Hint

Do not commit "crape murder"— topping the shrub or cutting its limbs back to the ground; the first produces an ugly, graceless plant, and the second a thicket of sucker growth.

Bloom Color
Red, white, pink, or lavender

Bloom Period
Summer

Height/Width
2 to 30 feet x 2 to 25 feet

Planting Location
- Moist, well-drained soil amended with organic matter
- Sun

Planting
- Plant in spring.
- Dig the hole twice as wide as the rootball and about the same depth.
- Add compost or finely shredded bark to the soil removed from the hole.
- Place the shrub in the hole, half-fill the hole with soil mixture, and water with transplanting solution.
- Fill the hole with soil mixture.
- Mulch with 2 to 3 inches of pine straw or fine pine bark.

Watering
- Water deeply when less than an inch of rain has fallen during the week.

Fertilizing
- When leaves appear, spread slow-release fertilizer for flowering shrubs at the base of the plant.
- *Or* spray with a water-soluble fertilizer in April and May.

Easy Tip
Look for the cultivars that have names of Indian tribes—'Comanche', 'Hopi', 'Natchez', 'Sioux', etc.—they're among the very best.

Suggestions for Vigorous Growth
- To increase the blooming time, remove spent blooms.
- After a normal winter, prune in early spring.
- After a severe winter, wait to prune until leaves appear.
- Gradually remove lower branches to expose the beautiful bark.

Pest Control
- Japanese beetles are the major pest; handpick them off, or check with a garden center about the latest controls. Do *not* place beetle traps nearby—they just attract more beetles to your yard.

Complementary Plants
- Plant several crapemyrtles together and underplant with *Vinca minor*.

Recommended Selections
- 'Tuskegee' eventually grows 20 feet tall and just as wide; it's cold hardy, has beautiful red blooms for over three months, doesn't develop mildew, and features colorful fall foliage.

Deciduous Azalea

Rhododendron species and hybrids

A Native Bloomer with Lots to Offer

Deciduous azaleas aren't as widely known or planted as their evergreen cousins, but they've been gaining ground recently. They're taller; the flowers are sometimes larger, intriguing, and often fragrant; and the leaves usually turn fiery in fall. Tennessee gardeners can choose from more than a dozen natives, with names like sweet azalea, pinkshell azalea, and swamp azalea. All are very hardy.

Top Reasons to Plant

- Showy spring blooms
- Wide range of colors
- Fragrant flowers
- Excellent fall foliage
- Pest and disease resistant
- Very hardy
- Attracts butterflies

Useful Hint

Deciduous azaleas offer a color range that evergreen azaleas can't provide—yellows, oranges, and creams—plus they're easier to grow.

Bloom Color
Yellow, cream, white, red, orange, or violet

Bloom Period
Spring to late July, depending on species

Height/Width
3 to 20 feet x 4 to 15 feet

Planting Location
- Moist, acidic, well-drained soil containing lots of organic matter
- Light shade to half sun

Planting
- Plant in spring.
- Dig the hole twice as wide as the rootball and about the same depth.
- Add compost or finely shredded bark to the soil removed from the hole.
- Place the shrub in the hole, half-fill the hole with soil mixture, and water with transplanting solution.
- Fill the hole with soil mixture.
- Mulch with several inches of pine straw or fine pine bark.

Watering
- Water regularly when plant is young.
- Thereafter, water when rainfall is less than normal.
- This shrub tolerates occasional dry soil but blooms better with regular watering during dry spells.

Fertilizing
- Fertilizer is not needed, but you can apply a mild, organic fertilizer, according to directions, in midspring.

Easy Tip

Filtered light—beneath tall trees with high limbs—is ideal for deciduous azaleas.

Suggestions for Vigorous Growth
- Don't shear these shrubs—instead use hand pruners to thin out wayward growth after the plant finishes blooming.

Pest Control
- Few pest or disease problems bother this shrub.

Complementary Plants
- For an excellent effect, mass together at the edge of a woodland or beneath tall pines.

Recommended Selections
- I like swamp azalea (*Rhododendron viscosum*) because it grows in wet places; it's hardy to -25 degrees Fahrenheit and has white or pink flowers.

Doublefile Viburnum
Viburnum plicatum

A Terrific Spring Performer with a Unique Look

There are a great many excellent viburnums, but this one deserves special attention. Many people consider doublefile viburnum the most gorgeous of all flowering shrubs—and that's saying a lot. This showy beauty has horizontal branches blanketed in spring with creamy-white or pink flowers lying in double rows along the branch tops, even in partly shady areas. The show returns in late summer with bright-red berries turning black in fall.

Top Reasons to Plant

- Beautiful spring blooms
- Unusual horizontal branching structure
- Red berries in late summer
- Burgundy foliage in fall
- Attracts birds
- Blooms well in partial shade
- Few pests or diseases

Useful Hint

Plant doublefile viburnum where it has room to grow and show off—do not interfere with the natural shape of this wide-spreading shrub.

38

Bloom Color
White or pink

Bloom Period
Mid-spring

Height/Width
8 to 10 feet x 8 to 10 feet

Planting Location
- Moist, well-drained, slightly acidic soil with lots of organic matter
- Sun to partial shade

Planting
- Plant in early spring or early fall.
- Dig the hole twice as wide as the rootball and about the same depth.
- Add compost or finely shredded bark to the soil removed from the hole.
- Place the shrub in the hole, half-fill the hole with soil mixture, and water with transplanting solution.
- Fill the hole with soil mixture.
- Mulch with 2 to 3 inches of pine straw or fine pine bark.

Watering
- Water regularly until the plant is well established.
- Once the shrub becomes established, water deeply during summer dry spells.

Fertilizing
- Feed in early spring with slow-release fertilizer for flowering shrubs.

Suggestions for Vigorous Growth
- Keep mulched year-round.
- No pruning is needed—or desirable— except to remove broken branches.
- If growth slows in mature plants, prune after blooming to renew growth.

Easy Tip
Doublefile viburnum really glows against a dark evergreen backdrop where its flowers can show off.

Pest Control
- Watch for Japanese beetles, and consult your Extension Agent for controls if they appear—do *not* use beetle traps; they just attract more beetles.
- Stressed shrubs may be attacked by insects, so don't let yours become stressed.

Complementary Plants
- Use as a specimen plant or as a focal point in a perennial border.
- Group several for informal hedging or screening.
- Plant along the edge of a woodland, preferably where you can look down on them and appreciate their horizontal structure.

Recommended Selections
- 'Mariesii' has large, white flowers, raised about $1/2$ inch above the spring leaves.
- 'Shasta' spreads 10 to 12 feet wide but grows only 6 feet tall with large, abundant white flowers.
- 'Pink Beauty' has deep-pink flowers, with the color developing as the blossoms age—it's more upright in habit.

Evergreen Azalea

Rhododendron species and hybrids

A Southern Classic Beloved by Millions

Once in a while, I read that evergreen azaleas have become a cliché across the South. Well, that's one way to look at it. I prefer to believe we've found a plant that loves our climate and transforms spring landscapes into a fairyland of red, white, pink, and lavender. I simply don't think there's a more beautiful or useful shrub.

Top Reasons to Plant

○ Brilliant display of spring flowers
○ Evergreen foliage
○ Thrives in shade
○ Good for cutting
○ New varieties tolerate cold

Useful Hint

Select your azaleas carefully to ensure their colors are attractive with your house and with one another.

Bloom Color
Shades of red, pink, lavender, white, salmon, or variegated

Bloom Period
Spring

Height/Width
1 to 10 feet x 3 to 10 feet

Planting Location
- Rich, moist, well-drained soil amended with lots of organic matter
- Partial shade to shade

Planting
- Plant in spring.
- Dig the hole twice as wide as the rootball and about the same depth.
- Add compost or finely shredded bark to the soil removed from the hole.
- Place the shrub in the hole, half-fill the hole with soil mixture, and water with transplanting solution.
- Fill the hole with soil mixture.
- Mulch with several inches of pine straw or fine pine bark.

Watering
- Never allow azaleas to dry out.
- Water weekly when rainfall hasn't totaled an inch.
- Moisture is especially important in summer—that's when plants are producing next spring's buds.

Fertilizing
- Spray plants with water-soluble, acidic fertilizer at the end of March, April, and May.

Easy Tip

We sometimes lose evergreen azaleas during that especially cold winter every ten years or so, but the solution is to plant hardy types, such as Girard hybrids.

Suggestions for Vigorous Growth
- Maintain 3 inches of mulch year-round to hold moisture and protect from cold.
- Prune right after plants stop blooming.

Pest Control
- In wet years, galls may be a problem—pick them off and dispose of them away from the garden.
- In dry years, spider mites may occur—consult the Extension Service for controls.
- Lace bugs are a frequent problem in warm weather—consult the Extension Service for controls.

Complementary Plants
- Pair with dogwoods for a beautiful effect.
- Use as foundation shrubs for a north-facing house.
- Plant red azaleas near white tulips.

Recommended Selections
- People go nuts over 'Girard's Hot Shot', which has glowing, orange-red blooms and fiery fall foliage.
- 'Glacier' is my favorite white—it produces 3-inch blooms on 6-foot plants.

41

Evergreen Holly

Ilex species and hybrids

A Reliable Evergreen for Winter Color and Form

Evergreen holly shrubs aren't just smaller versions of the American holly tree. The smooth, round leaves of Japanese holly (*Ilex crenata*) will remind you of boxwood, but it's hardier and much more disease resistant. Inkberry (*Ilex glabra*) is a similar native; both have inconspicuous black fruits. Chinese holly (*Ilex cornuta*) is known for red berries and glossy, prickly leaves. Don't overlook some of the hybrids, such as 'Fosteri', which can be kept pruned to size.

Top Reasons to Plant

- Evergreen foliage
- Showy red berries on some species
- Pest and disease resistant
- Cold tolerant
- Good cut greens for holiday decorations

Useful Hint

Japanese hollies (*Ilex crenata*) make a good stand-in for boxwood for hedges and screens.

Bloom Color
Inconspicuous white blooms, followed by red berries in fall on some species

Bloom Period
Spring

Height/Width
1 to 8 feet x 4 to 15 feet

Planting Location
- Well-drained, slightly acidic soil enriched with organic matter
- Sun or very light shade—Japanese holly does fine in partial shade, though the shadier the site, the slower it grows

Planting
- Plant in spring.
- Dig the hole twice as wide as the rootball and about the same depth.
- Add compost or finely shredded bark to the soil removed from the hole.
- Place the shrub in the hole, half-fill the hole with soil mixture, and water with transplanting solution.
- Fill the hole with soil mixture.
- Mulch with several inches of pine straw or fine pine bark.

Watering
- For the first two or three years, keep hollies watered when rainfall is below an inch per week.
- Once established, Chinese holly can tolerate drought and heat.

Fertilizing
- Feed yearly in spring with a slow-release shrub fertilizer such as Holly-tone®.

Easy Tip
Before you buy, learn the eventual height and width of the holly you're considering—then you won't have to spend hours pruning overgrown specimens that cover up the living room window.

Suggestions for Vigorous Growth
- Prune in December for holiday decorations.

Pest Control
- Inkberry has few pests.
- Spider mites may trouble Japanese holly.
- Scale may appear on Chinese holly.

Complementary Plants
- Depending on the type, plant as hedges and barriers.
- Use in foundation plantings.
- Use for topiaries.

Recommended Selections
- *Ilex cornuta* 'Carissa' has only a small spine on the ends of its leaves.
- *Ilex x aquipernyi* 'September Gem' fruits very early.
- *Ilex crenata* 'Beehive' is a compact, mounded plant that's hardy.
- *Ilex glabra* 'Green Billow' makes a nice ground cover.

False Cypress

Chamaecyparis species and hybrids

Excellent Needled Evergreens with Interesting Shapes

Why grow a shrub whose name you can't pronounce? Well, it increases your choice of needled evergreens. Then there's the interesting appearance—upright or drooping, dwarf or 50 feet tall, needles of green or gold. The main useful species are Hinoki false cypress (*Chamaecyparis obtusa*) and Sawara false cypress (*Chamaecyparis pisifera*). Just be sure to read the plant's label to understand its eventual size. Oh yes, just say Kam-uh-SIP-a-ris.

Top Reasons to Plant

- Evergreen needled foliage
- Yellow or green needles
- Variety of shapes and sizes
- Few pests and diseases
- Striking specimen
- Many different uses, depending on type

Useful Hint

Match the type of *Chamaecyparis* to the spot where you need an evergreen shrub—short or tall? Upright or weeping? Green or gold?

Height/Width
4 to 20 feet x 6 to 8 feet

Planting Location
- Moist, well-drained soil enriched with organic matter
- Sun

Planting
- Plant in spring or early autumn.
- Dig the hole twice as wide as the rootball and about the same depth.
- Add compost or finely shredded bark to the soil removed from the hole.
- Place the shrub in the hole, half-fill the hole with soil mixture, and water with transplanting solution.
- Fill the hole with soil mixture.
- Mulch with several inches of pine straw or fine pine bark.

Watering
- Water when there hasn't been an inch of rainfall during the week, especially during hot weather.
- Soak the soil thoroughly when watering.

Fertilizing
- Feed with a fertilizer for evergreens at the end of November or with a slow-release shrub fertilizer at the end of March.

Suggestions for Vigorous Growth
- Shape regularly—it's difficult to prune an overgrown evergreen without causing bare branches.

Easy Tip

The weeping forms of false cypress look wonderful cascading down a slope or over a wall.

- In late winter, remove dead stems and needles from the shrub's interior.
- Pinch tips of branches in late spring or early summer.

Pest Control
- Few insects and diseases trouble this shrub.

Complementary Plants
- Dwarfs look good in rock gardens.
- Many work well in foundation plantings or shrub borders.
- Unusual forms make excellent specimen shrubs.

Recommended Selections
- *Chamaecyparis pisifera* 'Golden Mop' is a dwarf with a threadleaf form (corded branches) that can only be described as "cute"—in the nicest sense of the word.
- *Chamaecyparis obtusa* 'Nana' remains 2 to 3 feet tall and wide; it's a good choice in rock gardens.

Flowering Quince

Chaenomeles species and hybrids

An Old-Fashioned Bloomer for Earliest Spring

The earlier a plant blooms in spring, the more welcome it is. That's why flowering quince has been planted across the South for generations. For many, the fact that the bright-red flowers don't last much longer than a week or two doesn't matter a bit. This is a plant that welcomes spring, promising that warm weather and glorious summer are on their way.

Top Reasons to Plant

○ Vibrant early spring blooms
○ Long lived
○ Few pests and diseases
○ Good cut flower
○ Branches force well indoors
○ Drought tolerant when established
○ Almost indestructible

Useful Hint

Plant flowering quince where it can show off in spring but recedes into the background in summer—after it blooms, it turns into a plain Jane.

Bloom Color
Red, pink, white, or orange

Bloom Period
Early spring

Height/Width
2 to 10 feet x 3 to 10 feet

Planting Location
- Well-drained, acidic soil with organic matter added to poor soil
- Sun

Planting
- Plant in spring.
- Dig the hole twice as wide as the rootball and about the same depth.
- Add compost or finely shredded bark to the soil removed from the hole.
- Place the shrub in the hole, half-fill the hole with soil mixture, and water with transplanting solution.
- Fill the hole with soil mixture.
- Mulch with several inches of pine straw or fine pine bark.

Watering
- When the plant is young, water to keep the soil moist.

Fertilizing
- In early years, feed in early spring with a shrub fertilizer.

Suggestions for Vigorous Growth
- Unless pruning for use indoors, do any pruning after all blooming has finished.
- Renew an overgrown shrub by cutting one-third of the stems back to the ground each year for three years.

Easy Tip

Cut branches in full bloom for indoor vases, or cut branches just beginning to bud for indoor forcing in late winter.

Pest Control
- If aphids appear, wash them off with a blast of water and spray with insecticidal soap.
- If many leaves drop in summer, it's usually due to excess rainfall and humidity.

Complementary Plants
- Use for a deciduous barrier hedge— due to its thorns.
- Combine with early-spring-flowering bulbs in compatible colors.

Recommended Selections
- 'Cameo' grows to 4 to 5 feet, with double, apricot-pink blooms and no thorns.
- 'Texas Scarlet' has abundant red blooms on a spreading plant no more than 3 to 3$^1/_2$ feet high.
- 'Spitfire', an upright rather than spreading form, has the most vivid red flowers I've seen.

Forsythia

Forsythia species and hybrids

A Glorious Yellow Spring Show-Off with Graceful Habits

I'm not about to hide my enthusiasm for forsythia—or golden bells. Almost the first thing I do after moving to a new house is plant one of these graceful shrubs with the arching stems. I love the bright-yellow blooms and the fact that they appear very early in the season. People who don't like this beautiful plant have usually planted it where it soon became crowded. Give it room to grow, prune it correctly, and you'll have a harbinger of spring of which to be proud.

Top Reasons to Plant

○ Beautiful yellow blooms in early spring
○ Graceful form
○ Good cut flower
○ Excellent for forcing in winter
○ Resistant to pests and diseases
○ Tolerates variety of soils
○ Comes in wide range of sizes

Useful Hint

Plant forsythia where the flowers can be seen from the house and the street.

48

Bloom Color
Yellow

Bloom Period
Early spring

Height/Width
2 to 10 feet x 4 to 12 feet

Planting Location
- Moist, well-drained soil with organic matter is best but tolerates any average soil
- Sun to mostly sun

Planting
- Plant from early spring until fall.
- Dig the hole twice as wide as the rootball and about the same depth.
- Add compost or finely shredded bark to the soil removed from the hole.
- Place the shrub in the hole, half-fill the hole with soil mixture, and water with transplanting solution.
- Fill the hole with soil mixture.
- Mulch with 2 to 3 inches of pine straw or fine pine bark.

Watering
- When the plant is young, water to keep the soil moist.
- Once the shrub becomes established, water when less than an inch of rain has fallen during the week.
- Don't let this plant dry out.

Fertilizing
- If growth has been very slow, feed with slow-release shrub fertilizer in spring.

Easy Tip

Never prune forsythia into a round ball or cut off its top—prune it correctly, and you'll retain its beautiful, natural weeping habit.

Suggestions for Vigorous Growth
- More poor pruning occurs with forsythia than almost any other shrub.
- Do *not* trim into a round ball or lop the top off.
- After flowering is finished, cut one-third of the stems back to ground level each year for three years.

Pest Control
- Few pests and diseases trouble this plant.

Complementary Plants
- Plant large-cupped, gold-flowered daffodils nearby for a color echo.

Recommended Selections
- 'Spectabilis' has large, very showy flowers, though its 10-foot by 10-foot size isn't for everyone.
- A ground-cover forsythia, 'Gold Tide' grows about 2 feet tall and 5 feet wide.
- 'Fiesta' has gold and green leaves on a plant only 2 to 3 feet high.

Fothergilla
Fothergilla species

A Southeastern Native That Shines in Three Seasons

The advice to "buy plants that are interesting in more than one season" has almost become a cliché, but following it saves time, money, and space. There's no need to plant and care for three shrubs when one gives you the same effect. Fothergilla, a southeastern native, shines in three seasons: white, honey-scented flowers in spring; nice green or bluish pest-resistant leaves in summer; and some of the most spectacular fall color around. Might as well buy two!

Top Reasons to Plant

○ Showy spring flowers
○ Fragrant blossoms
○ Outstanding fall foliage
○ Few pests and diseases
○ Easy care
○ Excellent in naturalized settings

Useful Hint

Flowers appear before the leaves on the dwarf species *Fothergilla gardenii* and with the foliage on *Fothergilla major*.

Bloom Color
White

Bloom Period
April and May

Height/Width
2 to 10 feet x 2 to 9 feet

Planting Location
- Moist, acidic, well-drained soil with lots of organic matter—avoid alkaline or wet soils
- Sun or a little shade

Planting
- Plant in spring.
- Dig the hole twice as wide as the rootball and about the same depth.
- Add compost or finely shredded bark to the soil removed from the hole.
- Place the shrub in the hole, half-fill the hole with soil mixture, and water with transplanting solution.
- Fill the hole with soil mixture.
- Mulch with several inches of pine straw or fine pine bark.

Watering
- This shrub requires regular moisture all its life.
- Water deeply whenever total rainfall for the week is less than an inch.

Fertilizing
- Feed in spring with a slow-release shrub fertilizer spread in a circle on the ground around the shrub, beginning an inch from the trunk and continuing a foot beyond the tips of the branches.

Easy Tip

Fothergilla gardenii usually remains under 3 to 4 feet high and is excellent for small spaces.

Suggestions for Vigorous Growth
- Maintain mulch year-round.
- *Fothergilla gardenii* tends to sucker—remove unwanted suckers anytime.
- Pruning is rarely needed.

Pest Control
- Few insects or diseases bother this shrub.

Complementary Plants
- Use for a mixed-shrub border.
- Plant along the sunny edges of a woodland flower garden with azaleas, rhododendrons, and perennial flowers for a beautiful effect.

Recommended Selections
- The very hardy *Fothergilla major* 'Mt. Airy' features blue-green summer leaves and spectacular yellow-orange-red fall foliage.

Glossy Abelia

Abelia × *grandiflora*

An Easy-Goer with a Summer-Long Flower Show

Glossy abelia's great asset is that it comes into bloom in May or June and continues until frost. A rounded, multistemmed, semievergreen shrub up to about 5 feet tall, it has dainty foliage and small, slightly fragrant, funnel-shaped pink flowers. The leaves take on a purplish bronze cast in late fall and last until early winter in the coldest parts of Tennessee, hanging on all winter in warmer areas.

Top Reasons to Plant

○ Long season of bloom
○ Fragrant flowers
○ Dainty, semievergreen foliage
○ Purplish fall color
○ Pest and disease resistant
○ Attracts butterflies

Useful Hint

Abelia 'Sunrise' has gold leaf margins, and 'Confetti' is a white variation—both are stunning planted with crapemyrtles and coarse-textured evergreens.

Bloom Color
Pink

Bloom Period
May or June until frost

Height/Width
3 to 6 feet x 5 feet

Planting Location
- Well-drained, acidic soil with lots of organic matter
- Sun to partial sun

Planting
- Plant in early spring or early fall.
- Dig the hole twice as wide as the rootball and about the same depth.
- Add compost or finely shredded bark to the soil removed from the hole.
- Place the shrub in the hole, half-fill the hole with soil mixture, and water with transplanting solution.
- Fill the hole with soil mixture.
- Mulch with 2 to 3 inches of pine straw or fine pine bark.

Watering
- During the plant's first year, water well every two weeks in spring and fall, and every week in summer, unless there's been an inch of rainfall during the week.

Fertilizing
- Feed lightly in early spring with a slow-release fertilizer for acid-loving plants.

Suggestions for Vigorous Growth
- In late winter, prune back dead branch tips to outward-facing buds.

Easy Tip
Abelia is a great plant for foraging honeybees and it never needs spraying.

- Prune off winterkilled tips in early spring.
- Once the shrub reaches a pleasing size, maintain it by removing up to a third of the branch tips each year after flowering is over.
- Maintain mulch year-round.

Pest Control
- Few pests and diseases bother this plant.

Complementary Plants
- Use to cover a bank for an excellent effect.

Recommended Selections
- 'Edward Goucher' is a tried-and-true favorite, growing 3 to 6 feet tall, with dense, arching growth and lilac-pink flowers. It makes a good informal hedge or specimen.
- 'Prostrata', a low-growing, compact shrub, has smaller leaves that turn burgundy-green in winter.

Hybrid Tea Rose

Rosa hybrids

The Aristocrat of Roses

Hybrid tea roses are long-stemmed flowers excellent for cutting, with blooms that are large, high-centered, pointed, and semidouble or double. Many, like the exquisite and enduring yellow-and-pink 'Peace', are perfumed. They bloom repeatedly from late spring through autumn, performing best in cooler weather. Though they need lots of attention, hybrid teas are America's most popular roses, partly because of their endless variety.

Top Reasons to Plant

○ Unsurpassed flower for cutting
○ Wide range of colors
○ Outstanding fragrance
○ Elegant buds

Useful Hint

Before choosing hybrid tea roses for your garden, get in touch with your local rose society, botanic garden, or other expert to find out what does best in your area.

Bloom Color
All colors except blue

Bloom Period
Spring through fall

Height/Width
3 to 8 feet x 3 to 8 feet

Planting Location
• Well-drained, fertile, moist soil with lots of organic matter
• Sun

Planting
• Plant bare-root roses in early spring and container roses in late spring.
• Dig the hole 24 inches wide and at least 18 inches deep.
• Mix soil with equal amounts of organic matter.
• For bare-root roses, build a cone of soil in the hole and drape roots over it. Remove container rose from pot and place in hole. Set rose so the bud union is 1 inch above ground level.
• Fill hole with amended soil.
• Water with transplanting solution.
• Mulch with pine straw or fine pine bark.

Watering
• Apply an inch of water per week unless it has rained that much.
• Avoid wetting foliage—use soaker hoses, if possible.

Fertilizing
• Apply slow-release fertilizer after pruning or planting and again monthly until early August.

Easy Tip

If you're not prepared to do the work required for success with hybrid tea roses, explore some other choices such as landscape roses or old roses.

Suggestions for Vigorous Growth
• Keep mulched year-round.
• As buds swell in spring, remove diseased and damaged canes and the oldest flowering canes, leaving an open structure of four to five strong canes 5 to 6 inches long with the uppermost buds pointing outward.
• Remove spent flowers, fallen petals and leaves, and suckers as they occur.
• Cut roses and spent blossoms at a point just above a five-leaf stem.

Pest Control
• Ask the Extension Service about a program to control insects and diseases.

Complementary Plants
• Hybrid tea roses are most often grown in a bed of their own.

Recommended Selections
• Some fragrant favorites are 'Tropicana' (orange), 'Fragrant Cloud'™ (vivid coral-red), 'Double Delight' (white blushed a rich red), and 'Touch of Class' (a slightly fragrant pink, coral, and cream rose usually raised for show).

Hydrangea

Hydrangea species and hybrids

A Beloved Summer-Bloomer with Some Surprising Relatives

Everyone knows bigleaf hydrangea (*Hydrangea macrophylla*), which produces big pink or blue "balls" in early summer. But do you know lacecap hydrangea, which has more delicate, elegant blooms? Or peegee hydrangea (*Hydrangea paniculata* 'Grandiflora'), often grown as a small tree? 'Annabelle', a cultivar of smooth hydrangea (*Hydrangea arborescens*), has 1-foot blooms on a 4- to 6-foot-tall bush. Look them over; you'll soon think, "Why not one of each?"

Top Reasons to Plant

○ Beautiful summer blossoms
○ Excellent cut flower
○ Good dried flower
○ Thrives in partial shade
○ Few pests and diseases

Useful Hint

If your hydrangeas don't bloom, the buds were probably killed by a late-spring cold snap.

Bloom Color
Pink, blue, red, or white

Bloom Period
Summer

Height/Width
3 to 10 feet x 3 to 10 feet

Planting Location
- Moist, well-drained soil with lots of organic matter
- Sun or partial shade
- Within reach of the hose

Planting
- Plant in spring.
- Dig the hole twice as wide as the rootball and about the same depth.
- Add compost or finely shredded bark to the soil removed from the hole.
- Place the shrub in the hole, half-fill the hole with soil mixture, and water with transplanting solution.
- Fill the hole with soil mixture.
- Mulch with 2 to 3 inches of pine straw or fine pine bark.

Watering
- Regular watering is essential.
- In hot summer months, you may need to water twice a week if rainfall isn't adequate.
- Watch for signs of wilting—that tells you to water quickly!

Fertilizing
- Feed in spring with an acidic fertilizer if you want blue blooms, and lime the plant in fall if you want pink—this isn't always foolproof, and in any case, only works with the bigleaf hydrangeas.

Easy Tip

Keep in mind that hydrangea's love for water is right there in its name—"hydro," the Latin word for water.

Suggestions for Vigorous Growth
- If needed, prune immediately after bloom—except for smooth hydrangea and peegee hydrangea, which are pruned in late winter or early spring.
- Rejuvenate any hydrangea by cutting it back to a foot tall.

Pest Control
- No serious pests or diseases trouble this plant.

Complementary Plants
- Use in a mixed-shrub border for an excellent effect.

Recommended Selections
- 'All Summer Beauty', a *Hydrangea macrophylla* cultivar, is the hardiest cultivar, plus it blooms on this year's growth, so late frosts aren't such a problem.
- 'Blue Wave', a *Hydrangea macrophylla* cultivar, is a tall, beautiful lacecap variety.
- 'Nikko Blue', a *Hydrangea macrophylla* cultivar, is a Japanese selection 4 to 6 feet tall with reliably rich-blue flowers—if your soil is at all acidic.

57

Juniper

Juniperus species and hybrids

The Rodney Dangerfield of Shrubs

Junipers are shrubs that get no respect. They are common as dirt, tough as nails, and green year-round. They're sheared into balls, tortured into pom-poms, and given the toughest of steep slopes to beautify. If a broadleafed shrub performed this well, it would be hailed throughout the country, yet junipers are not honored at all. While they may be common, they get the landscape job done without complaint.

Top Reasons to Plant

- Evergreen foliage effective year-round
- Wide range of sizes and uses
- Durable and reliable
- Drought tolerant
- Needs little care
- Adapts to wide variety of soils

Useful Hint

There are many, many cultivars of juniper—read the plant information tag carefully to make sure the one you have selected is the size and shape you want.

Height/Width
6 to 12 feet x 3 to 15 feet

Planting Location
- Any soil as long as it isn't soggy— improve drainage by adding organic matter
- Full sun

Planting
- Plant balled-and-burlapped shrubs in spring or fall.
- Plant container-grown shrubs anytime during the growing season.
- Dig the hole twice as wide as the rootball and about the same depth.
- Add compost or finely shredded bark to the soil removed from the hole.
- Place the shrub in the hole, half-fill the hole with soil mixture, and water with transplanting solution.
- Fill the hole with soil mixture.
- Mulch with 2 to 3 inches of pine straw or fine pine bark.

Watering
- Water regularly for the first year or two.
- Thereafter, junipers tolerate drought.

Fertilizing
- Feed in spring with a slow-release fertilizer for evergreens.

Suggestions for Vigorous Growth
- Keep mulched year-round—the decomposing mulch provides gentle feeding.
- Promptly prune off damaged branches.
- Prune as needed to shape and control size in early spring.

Easy Tip

Be sure to plant junipers in full sun— in partial shade they'll decline slowly, then die.

Pest Control
- Mites may appear—use a water spray to dislodge them.
- Bagworms may be a problem on stressed plants—handpick them off.
- If tips die back in spring on young junipers, a disease called *Phomopsis* may be present—control the disease by removing and disposing of affected shoots.

Complementary Plants
- Use taller types for hedges, screens, or evergreen backdrops for showy, blooming shrubs and flowers.
- Low-growing types are excellent ground covers and slope-holders.

Recommended Selections
- *Juniperus chinensis* 'Blue Point' is an easy-to-find upright variety.
- *Juniperus horizontalis* 'Blue Rug' and 'Bar Harbor' are two low-growing, spreading junipers.

Kerria

Kerria japonica

A Cheery Yellow Spring Bloomer with Green Stems in Winter

About the time forsythia finishes its spring show, kerria takes over. You'll find two flower forms. The one easiest to find ('Pleniflora') has small, double, bright-gold blooms that look like little gold balls. My favorite cultivars have single, clear-yellow blossoms shaped like buttercups. Whatever the flower type, the shrub's stems—which have a graceful arching habit in the species and some cultivars—are green in winter, adding an interesting touch to the landscape.

Top Reasons to Plant

○ Bright-yellow spring blooms
○ Green stems in winter
○ Few pests and diseases
○ Thrives in shade
○ Spreads quickly
○ Good in woodland settings

Useful Hint

Some gardeners call kerria "yellow rose of Texas."

Bloom Color
Yellow or gold

Bloom Period
Midspring

Height/Width
3 to 8 feet x 6 to 10 feet

Planting Location
- Adapts to almost any soil
- Shade or partial shade to avoid leaf burn in afternoon sun

Planting
- Plant from late winter until August.
- Dig the hole twice as wide as the rootball and about the same depth.
- Add compost or finely shredded bark to the soil removed from the hole.
- Place the shrub in the hole, half-fill the hole with soil mixture, and water with transplanting solution.
- Fill the hole with soil mixture.
- Mulch with several inches of pine straw or fine pine bark.

Watering
- Keep the soil moist in the early years until the plant becomes established.
- After that, water in dry spells to help prevent stem dieback and to promote better blooming.
- Watering is probably necessary in rocky soils.

Fertilizing
- Do not fertilize—it encourages excessive growth.

Easy Tip

Kerria suckers freely and eventually forms large colonies if you let it—give it plenty of space.

Suggestions for Vigorous Growth
- Prune each spring after flowering finishes to remove dead stems and tips of stems and to control size.
- To rejuvenate an overgrown shrub, cut one-third of the stems back to the ground each year for three years.
- Dig or pull up any unwanted suckers anytime.

Pest Control
- Few diseases or insects trouble this plant.

Complementary Plants
- Plant a single-flowering type in woodland gardens with wildflowers.
- Place near a door or window where flowers and stems can be seen from inside.

Recommended Selections
- The delightful 'Shannon' has been trouble free for me.
- 'Superba' has slightly larger flowers.

Landscape Rose

Rosa species and hybrids

The Easiest Way to Enjoy the Beauty and Fragrance of Roses

Landscape roses often fulfill a gardener's desire for roses without employing a crew of landscape horticulturists. Easy-care plants like rugosas, Meidiland, Carefree, and Dreamland roses are a sure bet for superb hedges and informal plantings. They make great barrier plantings or no-shear shrub borders. The rugosas, commonly called Japanese roses, are large plants with stiff, spiny canes. Two other candidates for hedges are 'Bonica' and 'Simplicity' roses.

Top Reasons to Plant

○ Beautiful flowers
○ Fragrant blossoms
○ Disease resistant
○ Require little care compared to many other roses
○ Excellent for hedges and screens

Useful Hint

Rugosa roses have large, showy, orange-red rose hips in the fall; they're high in vitamin C and edible—if you haven't sprayed them with insecticides or fungicides.

Bloom Color
White, pink, rose, yellow, or red

Bloom Period
Spring or summer

Height/Width
4 feet x 4 feet

Planting Location
- Deep, moist, well-drained soil with lots of organic matter
- Sun

Planting
- Plant bare-root roses in early spring and container roses in late spring.
- Dig the hole 24 inches wide and at least 18 inches deep.
- Mix soil with equal amounts of organic matter.
- For bare-root roses, build a cone of soil in the hole and drape roots over it. Remove container rose from pot and place in hole. Set rose so the bud union is 1 inch above ground level.
- Fill hole with amended soil.
- Water with transplanting solution.
- Mulch with pine straw or fine pine bark.

Watering
- During the first month, water enough to keep the soil moist, but keep the foliage dry.
- After that, water weekly.

Fertilizing
- Feed with slow-release rose fertilizer in spring after pruning.
- Thereafter, feed only if the foliage looks unhealthy.

Easy Tip

Landscape roses are about as easy as rose-growing gets, so consider planting them if you're not prepared to maintain the more demanding types.

Suggestions for Vigorous Growth
- Prune lightly in early spring and remove spent blossoms when possible.

Pest Control
- Watch for powdery mildew and blackspot—if they appear, consult the Extension Service about controls.

Complementary Plants
- Plant in groups or as mass plantings.
- Place in front of a picket fence or beside a gate—they'll stop traffic!

Recommended Selections
- Try the new hybrids widely available at garden centers.
- 'Blanc Double de Coubert' is a beautiful, fragrant, double, white rugosa rose with good hips in fall.

Leucothoe

Leucothoe species and hybrids

A Graceful Evergreen with Clusters of Blooms in Spring

The various species and cultivars of leucothoe have in common broad, evergreen leaves on graceful, arching branches. This almost weeping effect is especially welcome in a shrub. *Leucothoe fontanesiana* grows 3 to 6 feet tall and wide and grows best in the cooler parts of the state. *Leucothoe axillaris* does well throughout Tennessee and stays about 2 to 4 feet high.

Top Reasons to Plant

○ Clusters of fragrant flowers
○ Reddish spring foliage on some plants
○ Broad evergreen leaves
○ Does well in shade
○ Likes moist sites
○ Graceful, weeping form

Bloom Color
White

Bloom Period
Spring

Height/Width
2 to 6 feet x 3 to 7 feet

Planting Location
- Moist, well-drained, acidic soil with lots of organic matter
- Sheltered from winds
- Partial sun or shade

Planting
- Plant from midspring until fall.
- Dig the hole twice as wide as the rootball and about the same depth.
- Add compost or finely shredded bark to the soil removed from the hole.
- Place the shrub in the hole, half-fill the hole with soil mixture, and water with transplanting solution.
- Fill the hole with soil mixture.
- Mulch with several inches of pine straw or fine pine bark.

Watering
- Keep moist—this plant develops problems if stressed by lack of water.

Easy Tip
If you like plants with reddish new leaves, buy leucothoe in spring to make sure you get a plant with this characteristic.

Fertilizing
- Feed in early spring with a slow-release fertilizer for shrubs.

Suggestions for Vigorous Growth
- Keep a 3-inch mulch year-round.
- Prune right after flowering.
- If plant becomes overgrown, cut back to 18 inches tall and allow to regrow.

Pest Control
- Leaf spots, caused by fungi, are fairly common—check with your garden center or Extension Agent about controls.

Complementary Plants
- Plant with rhododendrons.
- Use to hide the legginess of Carolina jessamine.
- For a pretty effect, plant on a hill where its drooping form is emphasized.

Recommended Selections
- *Leucothoe axillaris* 'Sarah's Choice' is about 3 feet tall and produces more flowers than any leucothoe I've grown.
- *Leucothoe fontanesiana* 'Girard's Rainbow' has coppery-pink new foliage.

Useful Hint
Florida leucothoe (*Agarista populifolia*, also sold as *Leucothoe populifolia*) may reach 15 feet tall, although it can be kept pruned much shorter—it's a good choice for warmer sections of the state.

Loropetalum
Loropetalum chinense

A Showy Evergreen with Burgundy Leaves

This is one of those "see-it-gotta-have-it" plants. Early one fall, I picked up a couple of loropetalums at a garden center, then stopped by to visit several people before I went home. In every case, those spying the colorful shrubs in the back seat of my car wanted to know what they were. Although there are green-leaf forms, go for the cultivars with deep-red leaves all year. They really liven up the landscape in any season.

Top Reasons to Plant

○ Burgundy to red foliage year-round
○ Delightful fuzzy blooms in spring
○ Graceful, arching form
○ Easy to force indoors
○ Fragrant flowers
○ Adaptable to varying light conditions

Useful Hint

Loropetalum is a graceful spreader that grows quite tall, so site it where you don't have to butcher its shape by pruning.

Bloom Color
Pink or white

Bloom Period
Spring (and sometimes later)

Height/Width
6 to 12 feet x 5 to 10 feet

Planting Location
- Moist, well-drained, acidic soil with lots of organic matter
- Partial sun

Planting
- Plant from spring until early fall.
- Dig the hole twice as wide as the rootball and about the same depth.
- Add compost or finely shredded bark to the soil removed from the hole.
- Place the shrub in the hole, half-fill the hole with soil mixture, and water with transplanting solution.
- Fill the hole with soil mixture.
- Mulch with 2 to 3 inches of pine straw or fine pine bark.

Watering
- Water to keep the soil moist around young plants.
- Older plants can tolerate some dryness but grow and bloom better, and resist cold winters better, if regularly watered in weeks without an inch of rainfall.

Fertilizing
- After a hard winter or after pruning, feed in early spring with a slow-release fertilizer for shrubs.

Easy Tip

Like its witchhazel relatives, loropetalum's branches also force easily indoors in late winter.

Suggestions for Vigorous Growth
- Maintain mulch year-round.
- Damage may occur at 0 to 5 degrees Fahrenheit—if so, wait to see whether leaves and stems regrow, and prune as needed.
- Prune to maintain graceful shape—do *not* lop off top of plant.

Pest Control
- No pests or diseases bother this shrub.

Complementary Plants
- Use as a screen or group several together.
- Plant against an evergreen backdrop to show off the foliage.
- To create a good effect, use in gardens with a red theme.

Recommended Selections
- 'Burgundy' is my favorite so far—its leaves truly live up to the name and are a wonderful foil for the hot-pink blooms that begin in spring and often appear once in a while until fall.
- 'Zhuzhou Fuchsia' is good for the colder parts of Tennessee.

Miniature Rose

Rosa species and hybrids

A True Dwarf Rose That Requires Little Space

Miniature roses are the best-kept secret in the rose world. They're true dwarfs and handle cold winters happily because they grow on their own roots rather than being grafted. They can be grown in minimal space and are available in a vast selection of colors and cultivars. Many of them have fragrance similar to their larger cousins. Like an intricate tapestry, these tiny gems lend a captivating charm to any garden area.

Top Reasons to Plant

- Jewel-like blossoms
- Fragrant blooms on many types
- Fits into small spaces
- Cold tolerant
- Does well in containers
- Good cut flower

Useful Hint

The climbing types of miniature roses make beautiful tree-form roses and are lovely dripping from containers—which should be moved to a sheltered spot during winter.

Bloom Color
White, all hues of yellow and pink, or red

Bloom Period
Spring to fall

Height/Width
15 to 30 inches x 12 to 25 inches

Planting Location
- Well-drained, fertile, moist soil with lots of organic matter
- Sun to light shade

Planting
- Plant bare-root roses in early spring and container roses in late spring.
- Dig the hole 24 inches wide and at least 18 inches deep.
- Mix soil with equal amounts of organic matter.
- For bare-root roses, build a cone of soil in the hole and drape roots over it. Remove container rose from pot and place in hole. Set rose so the bud union is 1 inch above ground level.
- Fill hole with amended soil.
- Water with transplanting solution.
- Mulch with pine straw or fine pine bark.

Watering
- Water weekly unless an inch of rain has fallen.
- Keep water off the foliage—drip systems or soaker hoses work best.

Fertilizing
- Feed regularly with a rose fertilizer according to label directions.

Suggestions for Vigorous Growth
- Prune in early spring when buds begin swelling.

Easy Tip
Miniature roses are prone to blackspot and spider mites, so if you're not prepared to spray, explore landscape roses, which require much less maintenance.

- Remove dead, weak, and discolored canes and crossing canes.
- Trim all branches back by about a third, enough to maintain a pleasing form.

Pest Control
- Miniature roses are prone to spider mites, if grown in containers, and may also develop blackspot and powdery mildew. Consult the Extension Service for control advice.

Complementary Plants
- Mass together for the best effect—individual plants are too small to be effective alone.
- Plant as a border for a perennial or shrub bed.

Recommended Selections
- 'Rise 'N Shine', a vibrant yellow, is fragrant.
- 'Minnie Pearl' is a lovely light pink miniature growing 18 to 24 inches high.
- 'Red Cascade' and 'Starina' are good for hanging baskets.

Miss Kim Lilac

Syringa patula 'Miss Kim'

A Lovely Lilac That Tolerates a Tennessee Summer

'Miss Kim' is a heat-tolerant, disease-resistant lilac that does very nicely in the heat and humidity of Tennessee summers. Its sweetly fragrant lavender-pink flowers float over the stems and fade to ice-blue. A more compact shrub than the common lilac (*Syringa vulgaris*), 'Miss Kim' grows slowly. Its summer foliage is dark-green, turning mauve-purple in fall. 'Miss Kim' is a better and more reliable choice than the common lilacs grown by our northern cousins.

Top Reasons to Plant

- Lavish blooms
- Fragrant flowers
- Compact size
- Disease resistant
- Withstands summer heat and humidity
- Blooms well without cold winters

Bloom Color
Lavender pink

Bloom Period
Mid- to late spring

Height/Width
4 to 7 feet x 4 to 6 feet

Planting Location
- Moist, fertile, well-drained soil
- Open area with good air circulation
- Full sun

Planting
- Plant in spring or fall.
- Space plants at least 6 to 8 feet apart to prevent overcrowding.
- Dig the hole twice as wide as the rootball and about the same depth.
- Add compost or finely shredded bark to the soil removed from the hole.
- Place the shrub in the hole, half-fill the hole with soil mixture, and water with transplanting solution.
- Fill the hole with soil mixture.
- Mulch with 2 to 3 inches of pine straw or fine pine bark.

Easy Tip

Many southern gardeners find that Persian lilac (*Syringa* x *persica*) performs better than the common lilac (*Syringa vulgaris*).

Watering
- Keep moist until the plant becomes established.
- Water deeply in weeks without an inch of rainfall.

Fertilizing
- No fertilizer is required, but for faster growth, apply a slow-release fertilizer for flowering shrubs in early spring.

Suggestions for Vigorous Growth
- Pruning is not generally needed.

Pest Control
- Leaf diseases are more likely in wet seasons, with overcrowded plants, and in shade.

Complementary Plants
- Use for shrub borders or mass plantings.

Recommended Selections
- *Syringa meyeri* 'Palibin' is similar to 'Miss Kim' with deep-purple buds opening to pink-white or violet—it also resists mildew.

Useful Hint

If you're determined to grow the old-fashioned lilac, *Syringa vulgaris*, keep in mind that in most areas of Tennessee, winters aren't cold enough to guarantee good bloom, and summers are so hot and muggy that you will likely find yourself fighting powdery mildew—try the Descanso hybrids, developed to accept mild winters.

Mountain Laurel
Kalmia latifolia

A Handsome Native Evergreen with Showy Spring Blooms

Mountain laurel is a tall, exceptionally handsome, evergreen shrub with shiny, leathery leaves that make beautiful holiday roping. In mid- to late spring, mountain laurel bears clusters of white, pink, or red variegated cup-shaped florets. The blooms of the native species you encounter in the Smokies are pale-pink, but the modern hybrids are considerably showier, blooming in brighter pinks, reds, and bicolors.

Top Reasons to Plant

○ Beautiful clusters of spring flowers
○ Handsome, leathery evergreen leaves
○ Thrives in partial shade or shade
○ Few pests and diseases
○ Good cut flower and foliage
○ Excellent naturalized in woodland setting

Useful Hint

Caution: Every part of the mountain laurel is poisonous to humans but not to wildlife—though mountain laurel is deer resistant, Bambi will still nibble it.

Bloom Color
White, pink, red, or bicolors

Bloom Period
Spring

Height/Width
7 to 8 feet x 5 to 6 feet

Planting Location
- Rich, moist, well-drained soil with lots of organic matter
- Partial shade or shade

Planting
- Plant in early spring or early fall.
- Dig the hole twice as wide as the rootball and about the same depth.
- Add compost or finely shredded bark to the soil removed from the hole.
- Place the shrub in the hole, half-fill the hole with soil mixture, and water with transplanting solution.
- Fill the hole with soil mixture.
- Mulch with 2 to 3 inches of pine straw or fine pine bark.

Watering
- Water regularly until the plant becomes established.
- Once the shrub is established, water deeply during dry spells—this plant does not tolerate dry spells.

Fertilizing
- Feed in spring with a slow-release fertilizer for flowering shrubs.

Suggestions for Vigorous Growth
- Keep mulched year-round to conserve moisture and to provide gentle feeding as the mulch decays.
- Remove flower heads as they fade.

Easy Tip
If mountain laurel's leaves turn yellowish, with veins remaining green, it probably has chlorosis from inadequate acidity in the soil—use a powdered garden sulfur according to label directions to increase the soil's acidity.

- No pruning is needed—mountain laurel recovers slowly from pruning.

Pest Control
- Few pests and diseases bother this shrub if it's grown in an appropriate spot.
- Plants grown in the sun are subject to serious leaf disease and insect damage.

Complementary Plants
- Plant at the back of shaded shrub borders.
- Use for naturalizing with rhododendrons and azaleas at the edge of an open woodland.
- Mass on a shady bank for an excellent effect.

Recommended Selections
- 'Ostbo Red' has intense crimson buds opening to pink.
- 'Bullseye' is one of several forms with flowers banded in red inside.
- 'Elf' is a slow-growing, smaller cultivar eventually reaching 4 to 6 feet tall with light-pink buds opening to white.

Nandina

Nandina domestica

A Heavenly Shade-Loving Evergreen with Clusters of Red Berries—Or Is It?

When talking about nandina, it's almost as though you're speaking of two different shrubs. One is an old Southern favorite with delicate foliage, long clusters of berries on tall bamboolike stems, and a preference for shade. The other nandina is a small, round ball that tolerates sun, doesn't bloom or produce berries, and has brilliant fall color. One shrub—two types—lots of uses!

Top Reasons to Plant

- Beautiful, showy clusters of red berries
- Delicate, airy foliage
- Bamboolike appearance
- Evergreen foliage
- Thrives in shade
- Mounded, small habit
- Fiery autumn leaves
- Tolerates sun

Bloom Color
White followed by red berries on upright types—dwarf types generally don't bloom or bear berries

Bloom Period
Spring, with berries in fall lasting all winter

Height/Width
1 to 8 feet x 2 to 4 feet

Planting Location
- Rich, moist, well-drained soil with lots of organic matter
- Shade or partial shade for upright types
- Sun to light shade for dwarf types

Planting
- Plant in spring.
- Dig the hole twice as wide as the rootball and about the same depth.
- Add compost or finely shredded bark to the soil removed from the hole.
- Place the shrub in the hole, half-fill the hole with soil mixture, and water with transplanting solution.
- Fill the hole with soil mixture.
- Mulch with several inches of pine straw or fine pine bark.

Watering
- Keep soil moist, if possible, although mature plants can withstand dryness if in shade.

Useful Hint
Nandinas bear heavier crops of berries if several are grouped together—or at least several are in the neighborhood.

Easy Tip
Both types of nandina resist pests and diseases.

Fertilizing
- Feed in April with a slow-release fertilizer for shrubs—at half the recommended rate.

Suggestions for Vigorous Growth
- Dwarf, mounded types need little pruning—just snip off winter damage and maintain the round form.
- When upright nandinas become crowded, cut one-third of the canes back to the ground each year for three years—do this in early spring to avoid eliminating next year's berries.

Pest Control
- No serious pest or disease problems bother this plant.

Complementary Plants
- Use upright nandinas for screening or as a not-too-tall hedge.
- Use mounding nandinas for edging.

Recommended Selections
- 'Alba' has an abundance of white berries on an upright plant.
- 'Harbour Dwarf' is my favorite low-growing nandina.

Oakleaf Hydrangea

Hydrangea quercifolia

The Queen of Shade-Loving Shrubs

Oakleaf hydrangea has enormous, cone-shaped, white blooms that really put on a show in shade. Its large leaves closely resemble those of the red oak, hence its name. Oakleaf hydrangea provides the woodland garden with a lush, almost tropical, appeal. This deciduous shrub has outstanding cinnamon-colored peeling bark and wide-spreading branches. If you have enough space for it, definitely put an oakleaf hydrangea in your shade garden.

Top Reasons to Plant

○ Beautiful, huge summer blooms
○ Large, tropical-looking leaves
○ Striking bark in winter
○ Thrives in shade
○ Disease and pest resistant
○ Excellent for beginning gardeners
○ Good cut or dried flower

Useful Hint

If oak leaf hydrangea's big leaves wilt, don't despair—if you water right away, most times the plant perks right up.

76

Bloom Color
White fading to dusty-rose

Bloom Period
Summer

Height/Width
6 to 10 feet x 8 feet

Planting Location
- Rich, moist, well-drained soil with lots of organic matter
- Partial sun to shade

Planting
- Plant in spring.
- Dig the hole twice as wide as the rootball and about the same depth.
- Add compost or finely shredded bark to the soil removed from the hole.
- Place the shrub in the hole, half-fill the hole with soil mixture, and water with transplanting solution.
- Fill the hole with soil mixture.
- Mulch with several inches of pine straw or fine pine bark.

Watering
- Regular watering is essential.
- In hot summer months, until the plant becomes established, water twice a week if rainfall isn't adequate.
- The mature plant withstands some dryness.
- Watch for signs of wilting—that means water is needed!

Easy Tip
Like all hydrangeas, oak leaf hydrangea loves water, so plant it where it's convenient to the hose.

Fertilizing
- Feed in spring with a slow-release fertilizer for shrubs.

Suggestions for Vigorous Growth
- Keep mulched year-round.
- In spring, prune to remove sucker growth at base.
- On established plants, remove the oldest branches every other year.
- Cut back spent blooms in winter after they deteriorate.

Pest Control
- No serious pests or diseases trouble this plant.

Complementary Plants
- Use in a mixed-shrub border in shade.
- Plant compact cultivars in smaller gardens.
- Plant along the edge of the woods.

Recommended Selections
- 'Snow Queen' has huge, erect, conelike blooms.

Old Garden Rose

Rosa species and hybrids

A Disease-Resistant Antique Making a Comeback

The old-fashioned roses are certainly making a comeback all across the nation, including Tennessee. Appreciated in many cases for their repeat flowering and their disease resistance, old garden roses are defined as those introduced before 1867. Descended entirely or partly from east Asian roses, the reblooming categories include Chinas, Bourbons, damask perpetuals, hybrid perpetuals, Noisettes, and teas. All will probably make you think of your grandmother's garden—and they offer gorgeous, fragrant blooms in early summer.

Top Reasons to Plant

- Beautiful blooms
- Delightful fragrance
- Many are disease and pest resistant
- Graceful form
- Good cut flower
- Relatively low maintenance—for a rose

Useful Hint

The old garden roses mix beautifully into shrub plantings and perennial borders, so there's no need to isolate these beauties into beds of their own.

Bloom Color
Shades of pink, rose, white, or crimson

Bloom Period
Early summer through early fall

Height/Width
3 to 9 feet x 3 to 6 feet

Planting Location
- Deep, well-drained, moist, fertile soil with lots of organic matter
- Sun

Planting
- Plant bare-root roses in early spring and container roses in late spring.
- Dig the hole 24 inches wide and at least 18 inches deep.
- Mix soil with equal amounts of organic matter.
- For bare-root roses, build a cone of soil in the hole and drape roots over it. Remove container rose from pot and place in hole. Set rose so the bud union is 1 inch above ground level.
- Fill hole with amended soil.
- Water with transplanting solution.
- Mulch with pine straw or fine pine bark.

Watering
- During the first year, water regularly to keep the soil moist.
- Water deeply, using drip irrigation or a soaker hose to avoid wetting leaves.

Easy Tip
Old garden roses typically have few problems with pests, so they're low maintenance compared to hybrid teas.

Fertilizing
- Feed with slow-release rose fertilizer in midspring and again after blooming.

Suggestions for Vigorous Growth
- Prune in early spring when growth buds begin to swell.
- Seal pruning cuts with white household glue to prevent rose borers from entering.
- Remove old, spent roses especially on roses that rebloom.

Pest Control
- Consult the Extension Service about a control program for insects and diseases.

Complementary Plants
- Use in a formal rose garden.
- Plant as a backdrop for perennials.

Recommended Selections
- Old roses that may flourish with minimal spraying include 'Old Blush' (pink), 'Duchesse de Brabant' (pink), and 'Mrs. B.R. Cant' (silvery-pink).

Oregon Grape Holly

Mahonia aquifolium

A Shade-Lover with Shiny Leaves, Yellow Flowers, and Blue Berries

The new leaves of the Oregon grape holly start out red-bronze-green in spring, become dark-green in summer, then turn a beautiful bronze-plum in winter. But in addition to striking foliage, in late winter or early spring, this plant bears clusters of small, sweetly scented, yellow flowers, followed in summer by blue-black fruits reminiscent of grapes. The mahonias all love the shade.

Top Reasons to Plant

- Attractive foliage year-round
- Clusters of yellow blossoms in spring
- Fragrant flowers
- Grapelike fruits in summer
- Few pests and diseases
- Thrives in shade

Useful Hint

The edible fruit of the Oregon grape holly is said to make good jelly, though I've never tried it.

80

Bloom Color
Yellow followed by blue, then blue-black, berries

Bloom Period
April

Height/Width
3 to 6 feet x 3 to 4 feet

Planting Location
- Protected from wind
- Moist, well-drained, acidic soil with lots of organic matter
- Partial shade or shade

Planting
- Plant in early spring.
- Dig the hole twice as wide as the rootball and about the same depth.
- Add compost or finely shredded bark to the soil removed from the hole.
- Place the shrub in the hole, half-fill the hole with soil mixture, and water with transplanting solution.
- Fill the hole with soil mixture.
- Mulch with several inches of pine straw or fine pine bark.

Watering
- Keep soil moist until the plant becomes established.
- Established plants can withstand dry spells.

Fertilizing
- Feed with a slow-release fertilizer for shrubs in early spring.

Easy Tip
An easy plant to grow, mahonia looks good all year—an excellent choice for beginning gardeners.

Suggestions for Vigorous Growth
- Keep mulched year-round.
- If shrub becomes straggly, cut tallest stems back to the ground after blooming.
- Root out unwanted suckers as they appear.

Pest Control
- Few pests and diseases trouble this plant.

Complementary Plants
- Plant as a backdrop for shaded shrub and perennial borders.
- Use with hellebores, rhododendrons, azaleas, and other shade-lovers.

Recommended Selections
- *Mahonia aquifolium* 'Compactum' grows to just 2 or 3 feet tall, with very glossy leaves turning bronze in winter, and is good for smaller gardens.
- Leatherleaf mahonia (*Mahonia bealei*) is beautiful if you have room—it's more massive, with arching stems, big leaves, and larger flowers and berries.

Pieris

Pieris japonica

A Harbinger of Spring with Cascading Clusters of Blossoms

Whether you know it as andromeda or pieris, this mounding shrub has chains of lightly fragrant spring flowers cascading over the plant's spreading branches. Its reddish bronze new growth unfurls into lustrous evergreen foliage. A common name for pieris is lily-of-the-valley shrub, as the tiny flowers resemble those of the popular ground cover. This durable and truly beautiful shrub begins blooming before winter passes and is a real harbinger of spring.

Top Reasons to Plant

○ Beautiful chains of flowers in late winter
○ Fragrant blossoms
○ Lustrous green foliage
○ Showy new leaves of reddish bronze
○ Excellent with azaleas and rhododendrons
○ Thrives in partial shade

Useful Hint

Pieris is a relative of rhododendrons and azaleas—it both looks good and grows well with them.

Bloom Color
White or pink

Bloom Period
Late winter

Height/Width
4 to 6 feet x 4 to 6 feet

Planting Location
- Moist, acidic, well-drained soil with lots of organic matter
- Partial shade

Planting
- Plant in spring or early fall.
- Dig the hole twice as wide as the rootball and about the same depth.
- Add compost or finely shredded bark to the soil removed from the hole.
- Place the shrub in the hole, half-fill the hole with soil mixture, and water with transplanting solution.
- Fill the hole with soil mixture.
- Mulch with several inches of pine straw or fine pine bark.

Watering
- Do not let the soil dry out.
- Keep the soil moist for the first three summer seasons.
- After that, water weekly when there hasn't been an inch of rainfall.

Fertilizing
- In early April, feed with a fertilizer for acid-loving plants, such as an azalea-camellia fertilizer.

Easy Tip
In heavy clay soils, consider growing pieris in a raised bed.

Suggestions for Vigorous Growth
- Prune to shape or to remove dead branches.
- Cut back individual stems immediately after flowering in spring.
- Excessive watering and poor soil drainage can cause root rot.

Pest Control
- If twig dieback appears, prune out afftected stems immediately.
- Lacebugs can be a problem—if so, consult the Extension Service about a control.

Complementary Plants
- Mix with azaleas, rhododendrons, and ground covers.
- Plant at the edge of a woodland for an excellent effect.
- Use as specimen shrubs near the front door.

Recommended Selections
- 'Variegata' has year-round interest because of its white-edged leaves.
- 'Compacta' grows 4 to 6 feet tall and blooms heavily.

Purple Japanese Barberry

Berberis thunbergii 'Atropurpurea'

A Reliable Red-Leafed Shrub for a Sunny Spot

Purple Japanese barberry is a favorite of landscape professionals because of its reliable purple to red foliage, offering a nice contrast in green landscapes. Its color holds throughout the summer as long as it's in sun, then in fall the leaves change to deep-amber. Over winter, the thorny thicket adds texture to the garden. Adaptable to soils and drought, resistant to pests and diseases, purple Japanese barberry couldn't be any easier to grow.

Top Reasons to Plant

- Reddish purple foliage all summer
- Tolerates heat and humidity
- Resistant to pests and diseases
- Withstands drought
- Adjusts to a variety of soil types
- Interesting winter texture

Useful Hint

Japanese barberry has spiny leaves and thorns, so be sure to wear gloves when working with it.

Bloom Color
Inconspicuous yellow flowers

Bloom Period
Spring

Height/Width
2 to 3 feet x 3 to 5 feet

Planting Location
• Prefers slightly acidic, well-drained, loose soil, but adapts to most soils
• Sun

Planting
• Plant bare-root stock in early spring.
• Plant containerized stock anytime during the growing season.
• Dig the hole twice as wide as the rootball and about the same depth.
• Add compost or finely shredded bark to the soil removed from the hole.
• Place the shrub in the hole, half-fill the hole with soil mixture, and water with transplanting solution.
• Fill the hole with soil mixture.
• Mulch with several inches of pine straw or fine pine bark.

Watering
• During the first year, water deeply in weeks with less than an inch of rainfall.
• Once established, this plant tolerates drought.

Fertilizing
• In early spring, feed with a slow-release fertilizer for acid-loving plants.

Easy Tip
Japanese barberry tolerates drought, urban pollution, and neglect, so it's hard to beat for a low-maintenance plant.

Suggestions for Vigorous Growth
• Maintain mulch year-round.
• Prune to shape in late winter.
• Overgrown shrubs can be cut back to 10 inches in early spring to rejuvenate the plant.
• Root rot is a problem in wet soils.

Pest Control
• No serious diseases or insects bother this plant.

Complementary Plants
• Use as a specimen in otherwise green plantings.
• Plant as a low border or hedge to deter pets and wildlife.

Recommended Selections
• The low-growing 'Crimson Pygmy' reaches only 3 feet high at maturity.
• 'Rose Glow' has excellent reddish purple foliage and is a bit larger.

Pyracantha

Pyracantha coccinea

A Bevy of Brilliant Berries— But Choose Carefully

Pyracantha is a big, thorny, wide-branching evergreen with fine foliage and lightly scented clusters of white flowers in spring. But it's grown for what comes next—huge, showy clusters of berries in brilliant orange or scarlet, sometimes yellow. Songbirds feast on the fruit and welcome the thorns as protected nesting sites. But beware of more than thorns—pyracantha is subject to scale and fireblight, so be sure to select a disease-resistant cultivar.

Top Reasons to Plant

- Beautiful clusters of berries in late summer and fall
- Fine-textured, evergreen foliage
- Pretty white flowers in spring
- Attracts birds
- Good for espalier or trellis
- Drought tolerant

Useful Hint

Determined gardeners who don't mind thorns turn pyracantha into gorgeous espalier specimens.

Bloom Color
White followed by orange, red, or yellow berries

Bloom Period
Spring, with berries in late summer and fall

Height/Width
8 feet x 8 feet

Planting Location
- Any well-drained soil
- Sun

Planting
- Plant in early spring before growth begins.
- Dig the hole twice as wide as the rootball and about the same depth.
- Add compost or finely shredded bark to the soil removed from the hole.
- Place the shrub in the hole, half-fill the hole with soil mixture, and water with transplanting solution.
- Fill the hole with soil mixture.
- Mulch with several inches of pine straw or fine pine bark.

Watering
- Water weekly during dry spells for the first couple of years.
- Once established, this plant withstands drought.

Fertilizing
- Feed in spring with a slow-release fertilizer for shrubs.

Suggestions for Vigorous Growth
- Keep mulched year-round.

Easy Tip
To avoid problems with diseases on pyracantha, choose from disease-resistant cultivars known to do well in your area.

- Prune after blooming if needed to keep the plant inbounds, but remember as you prune that the flowers you leave provide you with berries in fall.
- Do severe pruning in early spring before bloom.

Pest Control
- Fireblight and scab can be serious problems that destroy plantings—buy disease-resistant cultivars.

Complementary Plants
- Plant as espalier against a wall or on a trellis.
- Use a compact variety for foundation plantings.

Recommended Selections
- 'Apache' features bright-red berries that last well into winter and resists fireblight and scab.
- 'Fiery Cascade', with orange berries turning to red, has good disease resistance.
- 'Mohave' bears a heavy crop of big orange-red berries that last into winter; it resists fireblight and scab.

Redvein Enkianthus

Enkianthus campanulatus

A Nicely Behaved Charmer with Assets in All Seasons

There's something quite appealing about delicate, bell-shaped flowers. And when they're creamy and veined with red (or just intense red) and cover the shrub in spring—well, that's hard to resist. But that's not all redvein enkianthus has going for it. Its leaves, bluish green in summer, change to brilliant shades of red, orange, and yellow in fall. In addition, it grows—usually slowly—to a medium size that fits just about any yard. Very nice.

Top Reasons to Plant

- ○ Small clusters of delicate flowers
- ○ Pretty summer leaves
- ○ Showy fall color
- ○ Interesting horizontal branching habit
- ○ Few pests and diseases
- ○ Grows slowly to moderate size

Useful Hint

Enkianthus blooms on the previous year's growth, so don't prune except to remove dead or diseased branches.

Bloom Color
White, pink, red, cream, or light-orange

Bloom Period
Late spring to early summer

Height/Width
6 to 10 feet x 4 to 12 feet

Planting Location
- Moist, well-drained, acidic soil with lots of organic matter
- Sun or some afternoon shade

Planting
- Plant anytime from spring until early autumn.
- Dig the hole twice as wide as the rootball and about the same depth.
- Add compost or finely shredded bark to the soil removed from the hole.
- Place the shrub in the hole, half-fill the hole with soil mixture, and water with transplanting solution.
- Fill the hole with soil mixture.
- Mulch with several inches of pine straw or fine pine bark.

Watering
- This plant suffers in hot summers if the soil dries out.
- Water deeply at least weekly if there hasn't been an inch of rainfall.

Fertilizing
- Feed each spring with a slow-release fertilizer for shrubs spread in a widening spiral around the shrub's base, beginning 1 to 2 inches from the trunk and continuing to 1 foot beyond the tips of the branches.

Easy Tip
Plant enkianthus where you can see it from indoors in fall and winter to enjoy its fall color and interesting form.

Suggestions for Vigorous Growth
- Maintain mulch year-round.
- Prune if needed right after blooming stops.

Pest Control
- Few diseases or insects trouble this plant.

Complementary Plants
- Plant with rhododendrons and deciduous azaleas for an excellent effect.

Recommended Selections
- 'Rubrum' has intense scarlet flowers in spring and fiery fall foliage.
- 'Red Bells' has two-toned red and cream flowers and outstanding fall color.
- *E. sikokianus* has maroon buds opening to red bells streaked with shrimp-pink.

Rhododendron

Rhododendron species and hybrids

A Gorgeous Spring Bloomer for Anywhere in Tennessee

Many of us admire rhododendrons but aren't sure whether we can—or should—grow them in our yards. Gardeners in the warmer parts of Tennessee have heard rhododendrons do best in colder climates. All of us wonder if they aren't just for the mountains. Put those doubts to rest. Rhododendrons can be grown anywhere in Tennessee, as long as the soil is acidic, contains plenty of organic matter, and has good drainage.

Top Reasons to Plant

○ Beautiful clusters of spring blooms
○ Handsome evergreen foliage
○ Thrives anywhere in Tennessee if sited correctly
○ Few pests and diseases if cared for properly
○ Outstanding in woodland settings with high shade

Useful Hint

Rhododendrons are *not* full-shade plants—they must have at least a half-day's sun to bloom well.

Bloom Color
White, pink, red, lavender, or yellow

Bloom Period
Late spring

Height/Width
1 to 15 feet x $1^1/_2$ to 12 feet

Planting Location
- Well-drained, acidic soil that's half organic matter
- Sheltered from winter morning sun—which will burn frozen leaves
- Sun at least half the day

Planting
- Plant in spring.
- Dig the hole twice as wide as the rootball and about the same depth.
- Add compost or finely shredded bark to the soil removed from the hole.
- Place the shrub in the hole, half-fill the hole with soil mixture, and water with transplanting solution.
- Fill the hole with soil mixture.
- Mulch with several inches of pine straw or fine pine bark.

Watering
- Water weekly if rainfall hasn't totaled an inch, especially in hot weather.

Fertilizing
- At the end of March, April, and May, spray the leaves and ground with plant food for acid-loving plants.
- *Or* apply cottonseed meal to the soil in April.

Easy Tip
If you have heavy clay soil, you may plant rhododendrons in raised beds if you're prepared to water and feed them regularly—these plants don't tolerate poor drainage.

Suggestions for Vigorous Growth
- Trim off winter damage in spring as new growth begins.
- Prune lightly each year after blooming to shape plant—pruning an overgrown rhododendron isn't easy or always successful.

Pest Control
- The most serious problem is rhododendron dieback—consult the Extension Service for advice.

Complementary Plants
- Make rhododendrons the centerpiece of a woodland garden by surrounding them with ferns, azaleas, and wildflowers.

Recommended Selections
- 'Roseum Elegans' is absolutely foolproof in any garden, though it can take several years to begin blooming—give it plenty of room.

Rose of Sharon
Hibiscus syriacus

An Old-Fashioned Favorite with Late Summer Flowers

This is an old-fashioned, tall, spreading shrub or small upright tree with a profusion of flowers from July till the end of September. The blooms are about 4 to 6 inches wide with ruffled petals crinkled on the margins. Look for one of the new cultivars introduced through the National Arboretum—they are sterile triploids with a longer blooming season, and they set fewer seeds, a plus since the seeds can be a real nuisance.

Top Reasons to Plant

○ Blooms in late summer when few other shrubs do
○ Attracts butterflies and hummingbirds
○ Blooms on new growth so it can be pruned severely
○ Inexpensive hedge or screen
○ Drought tolerant when established

Useful Hint

If you plant one of the old-fashioned types of rose of Sharon, be prepared to pull up *lots* of unwanted seedlings.

Bloom Color
White, pink, lavender-blue, lilac, or deep-red

Bloom Period
July to September

Height/Width
8 to 12 feet x 6 to 10 feet

Planting Location
- Prefers well-drained soil with lots of organic matter though tolerates wide variety of soils
- Sun

Planting
- Plant in early spring or early fall.
- Dig the hole twice as wide as the rootball and about the same depth.
- Add compost or finely shredded bark to the soil removed from the hole.
- Place the shrub in the hole, half-fill the hole with soil mixture, and water with transplanting solution.
- Fill the hole with soil mixture.
- Mulch with several inches of pine straw or fine pine bark.

Watering
- During the first year, water well every two weeks in spring and fall, and every seven to ten days in summer.
- Once the plant becomes established, water only during prolonged dry spells.

Fertilizing
- Fertilizer is usually not needed, but in early spring you may lightly apply a fertilizer for flowering shrubs.

Easy Tip
Rose of Sharon blooms may be single, semidouble, or double—buy a plant in bloom to ensure you get the form you prefer.

Suggestions for Vigorous Growth
- Keep mulched year-round.
- Prune heavily in early spring, cutting back branches to a pair of outward-facing buds.
- To control height on a mature plant, prune severely.
- For a treelike form, cut lower branches from trunks.

Pest Control
- Rose of Sharon attracts Japanese beetles, which may devour leaves—consult your Extension Agent or garden center for controls.

Complementary Plants
- Use to anchor a corner of a mixed border.
- Plant as an inexpensive hedge or screen.
- Underplant tree forms with annuals, perennials, or spreading hollies.

Recommended Selections
- 'Diana' has big, beautiful pure-white blossoms.
- 'Blue Bird' has lavender-blue flowers.
- 'Minerva', 'Aphrodite', and 'Helene' are all outstanding National Arboretum introductions.

93

Smoke Tree
Cotinus coggygria

A Showy Performer with Big Billowing Blooms

Smoke tree, or smoke bush, has to be the only plant ever grown not for the appearance of its flowers when they're fresh and new, but for the spectacular show the fluffy flower clusters put on after they've faded. The big, billowing blooms remind me of cotton candy more than smoke. Seed-grown smoke trees have variable leaf color—'Royal Purple' and 'Velvet Cloak' retain their reddish purple coloration.

Top Reasons to Plant

○ Gorgeous, airy plumes of blossoms
○ Long-lasting effect
○ Striking fall foliage
○ Few insects or diseases
○ Grows well in poor, rocky soil
○ Requires little maintenance

Useful Hint

If you prefer smoke trees with reddish purple foliage, buy plants in mid- to late summer—some fade to green late in the season.

Bloom Color
Yellowish, turning to pink and purple

Bloom Period
Late spring, with "smoke" developing in early summer

Height/Width
8 to 25 feet x 10 to 20 feet

Planting Location
- Prefers loose, fast-draining soil, so it's ideal for poor, rocky ground— tolerates any soil except wet ones
- Sun

Planting
- Plant from early spring to early fall.
- Dig the hole twice as wide as the rootball and about the same depth.
- Add compost or finely shredded bark to the soil removed from the hole.
- Place the shrub in the hole, half-fill the hole with soil mixture, and water with transplanting solution.
- Fill the hole with soil mixture.
- Mulch with several inches of pine straw or fine pine bark.

Watering
- Keep soil evenly moist when the plant is young.
- Mature plants can tolerate drier soil— but water during hot, dry summers.

Fertilizing
- Fertilizer is not usually needed—but if you want to encourage new growth on the purple-leafed cultivars, use a slow-release fertilizer for shrubs at the end of March or April.

Easy Tip

Smoke tree leafs out late, so don't be concerned that it has died over winter if it has no leaves after other shrubs do.

Suggestions for Vigorous Growth
- Little pruning is necessary—or desirable.
- Trim any straggly stems in early spring.

Pest Control
- No serious insect or disease problems trouble this plant.

Complementary Plants
- Use as a specimen shrub sited where it can be admired.
- Plant as the centerpiece of a flower border surrounded by plants with silvery foliage and pink or purple blooms.

Recommended Selections
- 'Velvet Cloak' has maroon-red leaves that hold their color all summer and are brilliant-red in fall.
- 'Pink Champagne' grows to about 7 feet with green leaves and long-lasting, feathery flowers.

Spirea

Spiraea species and hybrids

Something Old, Something New for Tennessee Gardens

Gardeners of a certain age always associate spirea with bridal wreath (*Spiraea prunifolia* 'Plena'), a 6-foot shrub with graceful arching stems lined with tiny white blooms in spring and colorful foliage in fall. But anyone who's had landscaping done in the past five years probably thinks of a low, mounded plant (*Spiraea* × *bumalda*) with pink blossoms from summer into autumn. Both are excellent choices for Tennessee gardens.

Top Reasons to Plant

○ Pretty blooms in spring or from spring till fall
○ Good fall color on some types
○ Few insects and diseases
○ Tolerates variety of soils
○ Requires little maintenance
○ Many forms and colors

Useful Hint

If you plant or inherit a bridal wreath spirea, let it grow in its natural, graceful form rather than pruning it into a meatball.

Bloom Color
White or pink

Bloom Period
White types bloom in spring; pink types bloom from spring until fall

Height/Width
1¹/₂ to 9 feet x 4 to 8 feet

Planting Location
- Tolerates any average soil except those that stay wet and don't drain well
- For best results, enrich soil with organic matter.
- Sun

Planting
- Plant anytime from spring until fall.
- Space plants according to eventual mature size.
- Dig the hole twice as wide as the rootball and about the same depth.
- Add compost or finely shredded bark to the soil removed from the hole.
- Place the shrub in the hole, half-fill the hole with soil mixture, and water with transplanting solution.
- Fill the hole with soil mixture.
- Mulch with several inches of pine straw or fine pine bark.

Watering
- When the plant is young, water deeply whenever weekly rainfall measures less than an inch.
- Bridal wreath types tolerate some dryness once established.

Fertilizing
- Feed in spring with a slow-release shrub fertilizer.

Easy Tip
Spireas require little care once established and are excellent low-maintenance shrubs.

Suggestions for Vigorous Growth
- Prune *Spiraea* x *bumalda* and Japanese spirea (including *Spiraea japonica* 'Goldmound') in late winter or early spring before growth starts.
- Prune bridal wreath types very soon after flowering ends.
- Rejuvenate overgrown shrubs by cutting one-third of old stems back to the ground each year for three years.

Pest Control
- Numerous insects and diseases may attack spirea, but few are fatal.

Complementary Plants
- Mass mounded spireas.
- Plant bridal wreath with other spring-flowering shrubs.
- Try *Spiraea japonica* 'Shirobana' with *Hydrangea arborescens* 'Annabelle' and a host of colorful daylilies.

Recommended Selections
- *Spiraea* x *bumalda* 'Anthony Waterer' has bluish green leaves in summer that turn red in fall.
- 'Limemound' forms a ball about 2 feet tall by 3 feet wide.
- *Spiraea japonica* 'Shirobana' has pink and white blooms on the same plant.

Summersweet

Clethra alnifolia

A Very Fragrant Bloomer with Pretty Flowers—and Adaptable to Boot

Don't you love plants with a sweet aroma? I think flowers should smell as good as they look, and summersweet's pink or white flower clusters certainly do. They're appreciated by bees as much as by humans. But fragrance and pretty flowers aren't the only sterling qualities of this native shrub. It thrives in those wet places that many plants won't tolerate. It adapts to almost any light from partial shade to full sun, and it has excellent fall foliage. To top it all off, summersweet is easy to grow.

Top Reasons to Plant

○ Fragrant, pretty blossoms
○ Excellent fall color
○ Thrives in partial shade to sun
○ Tolerates moist soil
○ Few pests and diseases
○ Easy to grow

Useful Hint

Summersweet flowers are so fragrant that just one or two plants can perfume a whole garden.

Bloom Color
White or pink

Bloom Period
Mid- to late summer

Height/Width
4 to 10 feet x 4 to 8 feet

Planting Location
• Moist, acidic soil with plenty of
  organic matter
• Sun to light shade to half shade

Planting
• Plant from spring till early autumn.
• Dig the hole twice as wide as the
  rootball and about the same depth.
• Add compost or finely shredded bark
  to the soil removed from the hole.
• Place the shrub in the hole, half-fill the
  hole with soil mixture, and water with
  transplanting solution.
• Fill the hole with soil mixture.
• Mulch with several inches of pine straw
  or fine pine bark.

Watering
• Water regularly for best performance
  and abundant flowers.
• Do not let the soil dry out.

Fertilizing
• Feed at end of March with a slow-
  release fertilizer for flowering shrubs.

Suggestions for Vigorous Growth
• Prune in late winter before new
  growth begins—this plant flowers on
  new growth.

Easy Tip

This delightful shrub couldn't be easier
to grow.

• Little pruning is usually required, but if
  plant has grown too large for its spot,
  cut back one-fourth of stems to the
  ground each year for four years.
• Spreads by rhizomes (fleshy roots)
  and suckers—remove unwanted plants
  anytime.

Pest Control
• Few insects or diseases bother
  this plant.

Complementary Plants
• Plant with Virginia sweetspire on the
  end of a woodland.

Recommended Selections
• 'Chattanooga' features nice white
  flowers on a 7-foot-tall shrub.
• 'Hummingbird' has white blossoms and
  grows only about 3 feet tall with deep-
  green summer leaves and clear-yellow
  fall ones.
• 'Pink Spire' features pale-pink blooms
  that don't fade.
• 'Ruby Spice' has rosy-pink flowers.

Viburnum

Viburnum species and hybrids

So Many Wonderful Choices, So Little Space

There are so many viburnums—and they differ so much—that you could grow just viburnums and still have a tremendous amount of variety in your yard. One attribute most viburnums share is berries—much appreciated by both birds and people. The size and shape of the flowers vary, as do bloom times, but blossoms are generally white or pink. Most are deciduous shrubs, but some are evergreen. Doublefile viburnum (*Viburnum plicatum*) is one of the loveliest and, as a result, has its own separate entry in this book.

Top Reasons to Plant

○ Beautiful blooms
○ Sweet fragrance in many varieties
○ Showy berries in many varieties
○ Attracts butterflies and birds
○ Needs little maintenance
○ Generally has few pests and diseases

Useful Hint

The snowball viburnums are extremely popular, but there are many wonderful choices among viburnums.

Bloom Color
White or pink

Bloom Period
Spring to summer, depending on species

Height/Width
2 to 30 feet x 4 to 15 feet

Planting Location
- Slightly acidic, moist, well-drained soil with lots of organic matter
- Sun or some afternoon shade

Planting
- Plant evergreen types in spring, deciduous varieties from spring till fall.
- Dig the hole twice as wide as the rootball and about the same depth.
- Add compost or finely shredded bark to the soil removed from the hole.
- Place the shrub in the hole, half-fill the hole with soil mixture, and water with transplanting solution.
- Fill the hole with soil mixture.
- Mulch with several inches of pine straw or fine pine bark.

Watering
- Water whenever rainfall hasn't amounted to an inch during the week.

Fertilizing
- Feed in spring with a slow-release fertilizer for flowering shrubs.

Suggestions for Vigorous Growth
- Prune if required just after flowering.
- Remove water sprouts (vertical stems) as they appear.

Easy Tip

The viburnum family is large and versatile, so it's important to read the plant label and talk with a knowledgeable person at the nursery to find out what soil and light is needed for the plant you're considering.

Pest Control
- This plant has many potential pests, but they're fairly rare.

Complementary Plants
- There's a viburnum for just about any use—screening, specimen, shrub or flower border, or hedge.
- Plant in wildlife-attracting gardens because of the berries.

Recommended Selections
- *Viburnum* x *burkwoodii* has pink buds with white and sweetly fragrant flowers in early spring.
- *Viburnum* x *pragense* is the evergreen one that has grown best in my garden.
- *Viburnum carlesii* has very fragrant spring blooms and red fall foliage.
- *Viburnum dilitatum* has showy, bright-red berries in fall—look for the cultivars 'Erie', 'Catskill', and 'Iroquois', all of which bear lots of berries and have good fall color.

Virginia Sweetspire
Itea virginica

An Outstanding Performer That Demands No Attention

This is one of my favorite deciduous shrubs. Maybe that's because I'm a native of Virginia. Or because I have so many tall trees, and it fits naturally into a woodland garden. Or possibly it's my appreciation of its brilliant fall foliage. It could be the fragrance of the flowers, or the way it blooms after all the spring shrubs have finished. Or the fact that, once Virginia sweetspire is planted, it needs almost no attention from me. All I have to do is stand back and admire it.

Top Reasons to Plant

- Pretty flowers in late spring
- Fragrant blooms
- Showy fall foliage
- Tolerates wet soils and clay
- Pest and disease resistant
- Needs little maintenance

Useful Hint

I prefer to plant Virginia sweetspire in partial shade and in soil that's on the dry side; that way, it stays more compact and doesn't spread as much.

Bloom Color
White

Bloom Period
Late spring to early summer

Height/Width
3 to 5 feet x 3 to 6 feet

Planting Location
• Any average soil, but loves wet soils and clay
• Full sun to partial shade

Planting
• Plant anytime from spring to early fall.
• Dig the hole twice as wide as the rootball and about the same depth.
• Add compost or finely shredded bark to the soil removed from the hole.
• Place the shrub in the hole, half-fill the hole with soil mixture, and water with transplanting solution.
• Fill the hole with soil mixture.
• Mulch with several inches of pine straw or fine pine bark.

Watering
• For the first two or three years, water regularly to keep the soil moist.
• Once the plant becomes established, water deeply during dry spells.

Fertilizing
• Feed in spring with a slow-release fertilizer for shrubs.

Easy Tip

Virginia sweetspire grows largest in full sun but doesn't mind partial shade, making it a nice understory shrub beneath large trees.

Suggestions for Vigorous Growth
• Maintain a 3-inch mulch year-round.
• Prune if required just after flowering finishes.

Pest Control
• Few insects or diseases bother this plant.
• Spots on leaves are generally harmless.

Complementary Plants
• Grow with wildflowers and ferns.
• Plant beside a water garden or stream.

Recommended Selections
• 'Henry's Garnet', the best-known and most reliable cultivar, thrives in summer heat and winter cold and has excellent flowers and fall color.
• 'Saturnalia' has brilliant-red fall foliage.

Weigela

Weigela florida

A Foolproof Member of the Honeysuckle Family

Weigelas are dense-flowering shrubs with spreading branches arching to the ground in maturity. Cousins of the honeysuckle, their gift to the gardener is color late in the year and a disposition to thrive no matter what the conditions. The flowers are showy clusters of inch-long, tubular flowers covering the plant in late spring and early summer. Some have a slight fragrance, and some repeat a few blooms later in the season.

Top Reasons to Plant

○ Showy clusters of flowers
○ Attracts hummingbirds and butterflies
○ Blooms after most other spring-flowering shrubs
○ Vigorous in most situations
○ Graceful, arching form
○ Good fall color
○ Easy to grow

Bloom Color
Rosy shades of pink and crimson, or white

Bloom Period
Late spring to early summer

Height/Width
3 to 10 feet x 8 to 12 feet

Planting Location
• Well-drained, fertile, moist soil
• Sun for best flowering, but blooms with light shade

Planting
• Plant in spring or early fall.
• Dig the hole twice as wide as the rootball and about the same depth.
• Add compost or finely shredded bark to the soil removed from the hole.
• Place the shrub in the hole, half-fill the hole with soil mixture, and water with transplanting solution.
• Fill the hole with soil mixture.
• Mulch with several inches of pine straw or fine pine bark.

Watering
• When the plant is young, water deeply any week when rainfall is less than an inch.
• Once the shrub becomes established, water deeply during dry spells.

Useful Hint
The most ornamental weigela is the old-fashioned *Weigela florida* 'Variegata', whose leaves have a creamy-white margin; it has deep-rose flowers and grows to a tidy 4 to 6 feet.

Easy Tip
Weigela is a good choice when you're looking for a shrub that will do well almost anywhere with little help.

Fertilizing
• Feed in early spring with a slow-release fertilizer for flowering shrubs.

Suggestions for Vigorous Growth
• Keep mulched year-round.
• After branches leaf out in spring, cut back tips dead from winter damage.
• If branches of 'Variegata' revert to plain leaves, cut back to older wood.

Pest Control
• Few pests and diseases bother this plant.

Complementary Plants
• Plant in an evergreen shrub border where flowers and foliage stand out.

Recommended Selections
• 'Bristol Ruby' has ruby-red flowers.
• 'Mont Blanc' is a large shrub with somewhat fragrant white blooms.
• 'Wine & Roses' has three-season appeal—new foliage is fresh green, flowers are pink-rose, and fall foliage is glossy burgundy-purple.

105

Winterberry

Ilex verticillata

A Deciduous Holly with Glowing Sprays of Red Berries in Winter

With so many evergreen hollies, why would you want to grow one that loses its leaves in winter? In a word—berries! Bare branches are completely covered with red or orange—once in a while yellow— berries all autumn and into the winter. Another advantage is soft, nonspiny foliage. In addition to winterberry (*Ilex verticillata*), there is another native deciduous holly, possumhaw (*Ilex decidua*).

Top Reasons to Plant

○ Showy red berries in fall and winter
○ Attracts birds
○ Likes moist soil
○ Easy to grow
○ Few pests and diseases
○ Excellent for winter garden

Useful Hint

If the birds leave you any berries as late as the holidays, winterberry makes wonderful indoor arrangements—it's also beautiful out in the snow with a cardinal munching away at the berries.

Bloom Color
Inconspicuous white blossoms, followed by gorgeous berries

Bloom Period
Spring, with berries in fall and winter

Height/Width
2 to 18 feet x 4 to 10 feet

Planting Location
- Moist, even wet, acidic soil
- Sun or a little light afternoon shade

Planting
- Plant from spring until early fall.
- Make sure each group of female cultivars has at least one male—such as 'Apollo', 'Raritan Chief', or 'Jim Dandy'—to pollinate it.
- Dig the hole twice as wide as the rootball and about the same depth.
- Add compost or finely shredded bark to the soil removed from the hole.
- Place the shrub in the hole, half-fill the hole with soil mixture, and water with transplanting solution.
- Fill the hole with soil mixture.
- Mulch with several inches of pine straw or fine pine bark.

Watering
- For best berry production, water whenever there's less than an inch of rainfall per week.

Fertilizing
- Feed with Holly-tone® in March or April.

Suggestions for Vigorous Growth
- No pruning is required, though it's fine to cut berry branches for indoor use.

Easy Tip
Winterberries are all very hardy, large shrubs excellent for a natural landscape.

- To rejuvenate overgrown plants, in early spring cut one-third of the stems back to ground level each year for three years.

Pest Control
- No serious insects or diseases trouble this plant.

Complementary Plants
- Use in masses or to attract wildlife.
- Plant against needled evergreens for a beautiful effect.

Recommended Selections
- *Ilex verticillata* 'Red Sprite' is fun because it's small, growing to only about 5 feet, with large berries.
- *Ilex decidua* 'Warren Red' has glossy green leaves and produces a heavy crop of longlasting berries.
- 'Sparkleberry', a cross between *I. verticillata* and *I. decidua*, is perhaps the showiest of all the winterberries, bearing a heavy crop of large, scarlet fruits—it must be pollinated with 'Apollo'.

Winter Daphne

Daphne odora

A Demanding Diva That Pays Off with Divine Winter Fragrance

On a cold February or March day, a single bloom of daphne is enough to remind you that spring will come again. Even when very small, daphne cheers the soul with its delightful, pervasive fragrance. Though it needs very well-drained soil, just the right amount of sun, and careful removal of diseased leaves, daphne is well worth the effort.

Top Reasons to Plant

- Clusters of small rosy-pink flowers
- Delightful fragrance
- Blooms in late winter
- Thick, glossy evergreen leaves
- Good cut flower

Useful Hint

Careful attention to placing and preparing soil for winter daphne is the key to success with it.

Bloom Color
Rosy-pink

Bloom Period
Late winter

Height/Width
2 to 4 feet x 2 to 4 feet

Planting Location
• Very well-drained, fertile soil
• Sun but with midday shade

Planting
• Plant in early spring.
• Dig the hole twice as wide as and one and one-half times as deep as the rootball.
• Mix 1 part soil with 1 part coarse builder's or pea gravel and 2 parts fine pine bark.
• Place the plant in the hole so the top of the rootball is slightly higher than ground level.
• Water with transplanting solution.
• Fill the hole with soil.
• Mulch with several inches of pine straw or fine pine bark.

Watering
• Water often enough to keep the plant from wilting.
• Overwatering causes root rot—a usually fatal problem that is daphne's biggest enemy.

Easy Tip

Cut a few of the nosegay-type flowers and float them in a bowl with camellia blossoms for a wonderful February treat.

Fertilizing
• Feed lightly right after bloom with a slow-release fertilizer for shrubs—but *not* acid-loving types.

Suggestions for Vigorous Growth
• This plant needs no pruning.

Pest Control
• Poor siting and care result in problems with root rot and leaf disease.

Complementary Plants
• Use in the perennial border for a beautiful effect.
• Plant near a door where the fragrance and flowers can be enjoyed.

Recommended Selections
• 'Aureomarginata' has a white margin around each leaf.
• *Daphne* x *burkwoodii* 'Carol Mackie' is less fragrant but also less demanding.

Witchhazel

Hamamelis species and hybrids

A Wonderful Winter Spirit-Lifter

Imagine what it's like to look out the window in January or February and see a shrub covered with yellow, red, orange, maroon, or copper flowers. It's a sight that definitely lifts the spirits. And it often leads to planting more witchhazels—the various colors are fun. You might want to train some as small trees. But witchhazel isn't a one-season shrub—several species and cultivars have excellent fall color.

Top Reasons to Plant

○ Winter blooms in bright colors
○ Fragrant flowers
○ Good fall color
○ Easy to grow
○ Pest and disease resistant
○ Adaptable to varying soils

Useful Hint

The bark of the common witchhazel (*Hamamelis virginiana*) is the source of the liniment witchhazel.

Bloom Color
Shades of yellow, red, and orange

Bloom Period
Winter

Height/Width
6 to 30 feet x 10 to 25 feet

Planting Location
- Moist, fertile soil with lots of organic matter—good in clay soil
- Sun to light shade

Planting
- Plant from late winter till fall.
- Read the plant's label to ensure proper spacing for its mature size.
- Dig the hole twice as wide as the rootball and about the same depth.
- Add compost or finely shredded bark to the soil removed from the hole.
- Place the shrub in the hole, half-fill the hole with soil mixture, and water with transplanting solution.
- Fill the hole with soil mixture.
- Mulch with several inches of pine straw or fine pine bark.

Watering
- Water regularly to keep the soil evenly moist.
- In hot, dry weather, check twice weekly to make sure the soil isn't dry.

Fertilizing
- Feed in early spring with a slow-release fertilizer for flowering shrubs.

Easy Tip
Cut budded branches of witchhazel, take them indoors, and put them in a vase for winter blooms.

Suggestions for Vigorous Growth
- Maintain 3 inches of mulch year-round.
- Prune to control size in late spring or early summer.

Pest Control
- This plant has few or no pest problems.

Complementary Plants
- Plant near a water garden.
- Place where it can be seen and admired from indoors in winter.
- Try surrounding golden-flowered types with 'February Gold' daffodils and purple crocus.

Recommended Selections
- *Hamamelis vernalis* 'Christmas Cheer' flowers first in my yard.
- Among the excellent *Hamamelis* x *intermedia* hybrids, my favorites are 'Jelena', with copper blooms, and 'Arnold Promise', still the best yellow I've grown.

Gardening Basics

Gardening isn't difficult; even small children are successful gardeners. But, as with other hobbies, gardening requires paying attention to the basics—soil, water, fertilizer, mulch, and weather. Pay attention to those, and you'll have a landscape to be proud of. Here's what you need to know.

Soil

Soil Is the Foundation

It's hard to get excited about dirt. It's not as interesting as plants. It doesn't bloom; it just sits there, underfoot. But the soil is the foundation for all your gardening. If the soil is good (either naturally or you've improved it), then plants are going to be happy. If the soil is poor, plants won't grow well and will develop problems.

So the first step is to learn what your soil is like. Your nearby neighbors can probably tell you; so can the Soil Conservation Service office in your county. A simple home test is to pick up a golf-ball-sized piece of moist but not wet soil. Squeeze and then release it. If the ball of soil crumbles, it has a balanced texture. If it holds its shape, it's clay.

The Importance of the Right Conditions

If you've read about gardening at all, you've heard the advice about having your soil tested. That's wise counsel. All it involves is digging up small samples of soil from various parts of your yard, mixing them together well, and turning them in to your County Extension Service to be sent off for testing. The best time to do this is fall, when the labs aren't so busy and when—if your soil needs lime—there's plenty of time to apply it and for it to begin to take effect.

When your soil test results come back, you'll learn if your soil is deficient in any nutrients (and consequently what kind and how much fertilizer to use) and also the pH of your soil. What's pH? It's the measure of acidity or alkalinity of your soil. A pH of 7 is neutral—below that is acidic, above that is alkaline. In Tennessee, most of our soils are acidic, but some of us do live on properties with alkaline soil. Because plants have definite preferences for one type or the other, it's important to know your soil's pH level.

Because the ideal soil for most plants is moist and well drained, it's good to know whether your soil tends to stay wet or dry and whether it drains well. Clay soils stay wet longer than loam; sandy or rocky soils drain much faster than other types of soil—which is often good—but they need watering more frequently. Plants that are able to live in especially wet or dry conditions are noted in the descriptions throughout this book.

If you suspect that drainage is poor at a site in your yard, test to be sure. Dig a hole 6 to 12 inches deep and as wide. Fill the hole with water and time how long it takes for the water to drain completely. If it takes

15 minutes to half an hour, drainage is good. Faster means the soil doesn't hold moisture well, and slower means clay.

Improving Your Soil
Just because your yard has a particular type of soil doesn't mean you have to live with it. Instead, improve it with soil amendments. Organic matter, such as compost, not only lightens heavy clay soil and improves its drainage, but it also boosts the water-holding capability of lighter soil.

Other good soil amendments include rotted leaves, rotted sawdust, composted manure, fine bark, old mushroom compost, and peat moss.

If you're digging a new bed, spread 3 or more inches of compost or other soil amendment on top of the soil and till it into the top 8 inches of soil. Otherwise, improve the soil as you plant.

Water

How Much Is Enough?
The rule of thumb says most popular garden plants need 1 inch of water per week in the growing season, and many need its equivalent all year long. Unfortunately, the amount of rain that fell at your city's airport, or other official weather station, may not be the amount that fell on your plants. The only way to know for sure is to put up a rain gauge to assist in obtaining a specific measurement. In summer, when "scattered showers" are always in the forecast, I find that the "official" rainfall and what fell on my yard are rarely the same. If I had watered—or not watered—on the basis of the totals given by the National Weather Service, I would almost always either overwater or under-water my plants. Instead, I save time and money—as well as protect my plants—by knowing exactly how much rainfall they receive.

When and How to Water
In general, plants respond best to thorough but occasional soakings rather than daily spurts of smaller amounts of water. Regulate water pressure to reduce runoff so more water gets into the soil. Such good garden practices as these encourage plants to develop deeper roots, which provide greater stability; that's especially important for shrubs and trees. Deep roots also make plants more drought-tolerant.

The worst thing you can do for your plants in a drought is to stand over them with a hose for a few minutes each evening. Most of the water runs off instead of soaking in, and what does penetrate the soil doesn't usually go deeply enough. The soil should be wet to at least 8 to 10 inches deep for perennials and other flowers; 12 to 24 inches deep for trees and shrubs. Insert a dry stick into the soil to be sure how far the water has penetrated. It's impossible to say how long watering will take, because water absorption rates vary by soil type. An inch of water will penetrate fastest into sandy soil and slowest into clay. Time your watering the first few times and then you'll have a guide for future watering.

If you use sprinklers or an irrigation system, set out coffee cans at intervals to measure the amount of water delivered in 30 minutes. That will show you how long it will take the system to deliver an inch of water to your plants.

Too little water causes plants to perform poorly. Small leaves, pale or no flowers, stunted size, wilting, little or no fruit formation, and premature leaf drop can all be signs of water stress. Soil surfaces may dry out and even crack, destroying feeder roots near the surface; their loss can be fatal to annual flowers and vegetables. If watering seems adequate and plants still wilt daily, they may be located in too much sun. If such beds are deeply mulched, check to be certain that the water is getting down into the soil.

The best time of day to water is early morning; late afternoon is second best. No one wants to get up at 4 a.m. to turn on a lawn sprinkler. But there's an easy way out. Water timers can be attached to any hose and faucet to regulate sprinklers and soaker hoses; their effective use is the hallmark of in-ground irrigation systems. Soaker hoses—which don't wet foliage—may be used any time day or night.

The Right Tools

As with all gardening activities, watering is more efficient with the right equipment. Small gardens and containers of plants can be watered efficiently with only a garden hose and watering can—use a water-breaking nozzle to convert the solid stream of water into smaller droplets that will not damage plants. When watering container plants, irrigate until water flows out the drain hole in the bottom of the pot, and then cover the soil with water once again. This practice keeps the root zone healthy by exchanging gases in the soil.

Larger garden beds require sprinklers, either portable or in-ground systems. Sprinklers spread plenty of water around and most of it gets to soil level; the rest is lost to evaporation but does provide a playground and essential moisture for birds. Adjustable sprinkler heads are a good investment; the ability to set the pattern specifically to increase the size of the water droplets gives the gardener more control over irrigation.

Where water is precious or pricey, drip watering systems and soaker hoses offer very efficient irrigation. They're especially useful around plants, such as roses and zinnias, that develop mildew or other fungus diseases easily. These hoses apply much smaller amounts of water at one time than you may be used to. To measure output, let the water run for an hour, then turn the soaker hose off. Dig down into the soil to see how deeply it is wet. That will help you gauge how long to keep soaker hoses or drip systems on. For the health of your plants, when watering this way, occasionally supplement with overhead watering (either sprinklers or hand-held hoses) to clean the leaves and deter insects.

Watering Plants in Containers
Because hanging baskets and annuals in small pots often become rootbound by midsummer—when temperature and humidity levels are high—they may need watering once or even twice daily. You can lessen this chore slightly by mixing a super-absorbent polymer into the soil at planting time. When mixed, these look like Jell-O®. They absorb moisture, and then release it as the plants need it. Although they're pricey, only a tiny amount is needed (never use more than what is recommended, or you'll have a mess on your hands), and they last in the soil for up to five years. My experience is that they just about double the length of time between waterings. That is, if I would water a container plant without the polymer once a day, then with the polymer, I can usually water every other day. That may not sound like a big deal, but in the dog days of August it's a blessing! These super-absorbent polymers are sold under a number of trade names; ask for them at garden centers and nurseries.

Why Is Watering Important?
Water is vital because it makes up at least 95 percent of a plant's mass, and its timely supply is crucial to healthy growth. It is literally the elixir of life, moving from the root zone and leaf surfaces into the plant's systems, carrying nutrients and filling cells to create stems, leaves, flowers, and fruit. Without ample water for roots to work efficiently, nutrients go unabsorbed, growth is stunted, and plant tissues eventually collapse, wilt, and die. Ironically, too much water creates equally disastrous conditions. When soils are flooded, the roots suffocate, stop pumping water and nutrients, and the plant eventually dies.

Watering Tips
- Shrubs and other plants growing under the overhang of the roof may need more frequent watering than those planted out in the yard. Foundation shrubs often don't get much water from precipitation, and they also have to contend with the reflected heat from the house.
- Raised beds, berms, and mounds also need watering more often.
- Watch out for excessive runoff when watering. If the soil isn't absorbing the moisture, slow down the rate of water application.
- Never fertilize without watering thoroughly afterward. Fertilizer salts can damage the roots if moisture is lacking.

Fertilizer
Nutrition in appropriate amounts is as important as sunlight and water to plant growth. Three elements—nitrogen, phosphorus, and potassium—

are essential to plants and are called macronutrients. Some of these nutrients are obtained from the soil, but if they're not available in the amounts needed, the gardener must provide them through fertilizer.

The Role of Nutrition

Each nutrient plays a major role in plant development. Nitrogen produces healthy, green leaves, while phosphorus and potassium are responsible for strong stems, flowers, and fruit. Without enough of any one of the macronutrients, plants falter and often die. Other elements, needed in much smaller amounts, are known as *trace elements, minor elements,* or *micronutrients*. Included in most complete fertilizers, the minor elements are boron, iron, manganese, zinc, copper, and molybdenum.

Fertilizers come from two basic sources: organic materials and manufactured ones. Organic sources include rocks, plants, and animals; fertilizers are extracted or composted from them. The advantages of organics affect both plants and people: centuries of history to explain their uses, slow and steady action on plants and especially soils, and the opportunity to put local and recycled materials to good use. Manufactured sources are the products of laboratories. Nutrients are formulated by scientists and produced in factories. The advantages of commercially prepared inorganic fertilizers are consistency of product, formula diversity, definitive analysis of contents, and ready availability. Most gardeners use a combination of the two, but purely organic enthusiasts use natural products exclusively.

Speaking the Language

Every fertilizer sold must have a label detailing its contents. Understanding the composition and numbers improves the gardener's ability to provide nutrition. The three numbers on a fertilizer label relate to its contents; the first number indicates the amount of nitrogen, the second number the amount of phosphorus, and the third the amount of potassium. For example, if the numbers are 20-15-10, it means the product has 20 percent nitrogen, 15 percent phosphorus, and 10 percent potassium. Their relative numbers reveal their impact on plants—a formula high in nitrogen greens-up the plant and grows leaves, ones with lower first and higher second and third numbers encourage flowers and fruits.

A good rule of thumb is to use a balanced fertilizer (one where all the numbers are equal, as in 10-10-10) to prepare new soil. Then fertilize the plants with a formula higher in nitrogen at the beginning of the growing season to get plants up and growing; switch to special formulas (that is, those formulated specifically for flowers and fruiting) later in the season.

Fertilizers can be water-soluble or granular; both types have advantages and appropriate uses. Soluble formulas are mixed in water. They are available in very specific formulas, compact to store, fast acting, and can be used either as a soil drench or to spray the leaves (plants will absorb them through foliage or soil). Solubles work quickly (leaves will often green up overnight—great if you want the yard to look good for a cookout), but their effects do not last long and they must be reapplied frequently. They are especially useful in growing container plants, which need more frequent watering as well as fertilizing.

Granular fertilizers can be worked into the soil when tilling or used as a top dressing around established plants. They incorporate easily into soils, and their effects may last for several weeks. Slow-release fertilizers, which are usually pelleted, keep working for three to nine months depending on the formula. The coated pellets of these popular fertilizers (with names like Osmocote, Polyon, and Once) decompose slowly with water or temperature changes over time. They cost more than granular fertilizers but save much time for the gardener because they're usually applied just once a season. Their other big advantage over granular fertilizers is that it's almost impossible for gardeners to "burn" plant foliage when using them; whereas, great care must be taken to keep granular fertilizers off plant parts.

Organic fertilizers also work very slowly, over a long period of time. They usually have lower ratios of active ingredients (nitrogen, phosphorus, and potassium) and so provide steady nutrition, rather than a quick green-up. Organic fertilizers that provide nitrogen are bloodmeal, fishmeal, soybean meal, and cottonseed meal. Organic phosphorous fertilizers include bonemeal and rock phosphate. To provide potassium, use greensand or sulfate of potash-magnesia.

Although soil may contain many nutrients, most gardeners find applying fertilizer makes growing plants more satisfactory. However, many tend to overdo it. Too much fertilizer can harm plants, just as too little does. Excessive nitrogen often leads to attacks of aphids, which appreciate the tender young growth that's being produced, and to floppy stems in perennial plants.

Rules to Remember
- Never fertilize a dry plant. Water the day before you fertilize at least, or several hours before.
- Always use products at the recommended rate or a bit lower. Never use more than what is recommended.
- Rinse stray granules off plant leaves to prevent burning.

Mulch

One important thing you can provide your plants—which may mean the difference between success and failure—is mulch.

Mulch Matters

Mulch is the most useful material in your garden. A blanket of mulch keeps soil warmer in winter and cooler in summer, prevents erosion, and doesn't allow the soil surface to develop a hard crust. When heavy rain or drought causes water stress, mulch ameliorates both situations, acting as a barrier to flooding and conserving water in dry soil. Mulch suppresses weed growth and prevents soil from splashing onto leaves (and thus reduces the spread of soilborne diseases). A neat circle of mulch around newly planted trees offers a physical barrier to keep lawnmowers and string trimmers away from tender trunks. (Such trunk damage is one of the leading causes of death for young trees.) Mulch also makes a garden look neater than it does with just bare soil.

What Mulch Is

Mulch can be any material, organic or inorganic, that covers the soil's surface. Popular organic mulches include hardwood barks (ground, shredded, or nuggets), pine and wheat straws, shredded leaves and leaf mold, and shredded newsprint and other papers. Your excess grass clippings also make a great mulch, provided you let them age a week or so (until they're no longer hot) before using, so they don't burn plants. Organic mulches gradually break down and enrich the soil.

If you can find a source of free organic material in your area—peanut hulls, ground-up corncobs, waste from an old cotton gin, or similar materials—so much the better. I have a friend who's a high school industrial arts teacher, and several times a year he brings me enormous bags of sawdust, left over from his students' projects. Some of it I let rot and use as a soil amendment, but I also spread quite a bit of the fresh sawdust around all sorts of plants as mulch.

And, of course, don't overlook rotted leaves as an excellent no-cost mulch. I've often wondered why some homeowners lug bags of leaves to the curb in fall, then, in spring, turn around and spend money to buy bags and bales of mulch material from a nursery.

Inorganic mulches can be made from pea gravel, crushed lava rock, marble chips, crushed pottery chards, and clear or black plastic. Also available in garden centers to be used as mulch are rolls of landscape fabric, which look like a thick cloth. Both plastic and landscape fabric need to be covered with a layer of an organic mulch for appearance's sake, unless used in the vegetable garden.

In general, organic mulches are best around your yard's ornamental plantings. Black plastic and some landscape fabrics can prevent air, water, and nutrients from readily reaching the roots of your plants. They also cause shallow root growth, which makes the plants more susceptible to drought.

Because pea gravel and other stone mulches are difficult to move if you decide you don't like the way they look, you may want to try them in a small spot first. They're ideal, however, for pathways and other permanent areas, because they don't rot or float away.

What Can Mulch Do?

Beyond practical considerations, you may want to think about what different mulch materials offer the landscape aesthetically. The color and texture of many mulches can be attractive and offer contrast to green plants and lawns. Used on walkways and paths, mulch should provide a comfortable walking surface in addition to adding color and weed control to high-traffic areas. Mulch adds definition to planting areas and can be extended to neatly cover thinning lawn areas under trees. Mulch also works as a landscape-unifying element—use the same mulch material throughout the garden to tie diverse plantings together visually and to reduce maintenance at the same time.

Mulch Dos and Don'ts

- Apply mulch 3 inches deep when planting new trees and shrubs.
- Replenish mulch around perennials each year when tending established beds in spring or fall. Apply pine straw to a depth of about 5 inches because it quickly settles.
- Use pine straw to mulch plantings on slopes or hills, where other mulches may be washed away in hard rains.
- Don't pile mulch against a plant's stem or trunk; that can cause damage. Instead, start spreading mulch about 2 inches away from the plant.
- Don't pile mounds of mulch around trees; it's not good for them.
- When setting out small bedding plants, you may find it easier to mulch the entire bed first—then dig individual holes—rather than to try to spread mulch evenly around tiny seedlings.
- Don't spread mulch over weed-infested ground, thinking it will kill the weeds. Generally, they'll pop right through. Instead, weed before mulching.
- Add to the organic mulch around each plant yearly—9 to 12 months after you originally mulched. Think of this mulch renewal not as a chore, but as a garden job that pays rich dividends.
- In fall always add more mulch around plants that may be damaged by an extra-cold winter.
- Wait until the soil has reliably warmed up (usually in May sometime) before mulching heat-loving plants, such as perennial hibiscus, caladium, and Madagascar periwinkle. If they're mulched too early, the soil will remain cool and they'll get off to a very slow start.
- Don't mulch ground that stays wet all the time.
- Don't over-do the mulch. More than 4 or 5 inches of mulch may prevent water from penetrating to the soil below.

Glossary

Alkaline soil: soil with a pH greater than 7.0. It lacks acidity, often because it has limestone in it.

All-purpose fertilizer: powdered, liquid, or granular fertilizer with a balanced proportion of the three key nutrients—nitrogen (N), phosphorus (P), and potassium (K). It is suitable for maintenance nutrition for most plants.

Annual: a plant that lives its entire life in one season. It is genetically determined to germinate, grow, flower, set seed, and die the same year.

Balled and burlapped: describes a tree or shrub grown in the field whose soilball was wrapped with protective burlap and twine when the plant was dug up to be sold or transplanted.

Bare root: describes plants that have been packaged without any soil around their roots. (Often young shrubs and trees purchased through the mail arrive with their exposed roots covered with moist peat or sphagnum moss, sawdust, or similar material, and wrapped in plastic.)

Barrier plant: a plant that has intimidating thorns or spines and is sited purposely to block foot traffic or other access to the home or yard.

Beneficial insects: insects or their larvae that prey on pest organisms and their eggs. They may be flying insects, such as ladybugs, parasitic wasps, praying mantids, and soldier bugs, or soil dwellers such as predatory nematodes, spiders, and ants.

Berm: a narrow, raised ring of soil around a tree, used to hold water so it will be directed to the root zone.

Bract: a modified leaf structure on a plant stem near its flower, resembling a petal. Often it is more colorful and visible than the actual flower, as in dogwood.

Bud union: the place where the top of a plant was grafted to the rootstock; usually refers to roses.

Canopy: the overhead branching area of a tree, usually referring to its extent including foliage.

Cold hardiness: the ability of a perennial plant to survive the winter cold in a particular area.

Composite: a flower that is actually composed of many tiny flowers. Typically, they are flat clusters of tiny, tight florets, sometimes surrounded by wider-petaled florets. Composite flowers are highly attractive to bees and beneficial insects.

Compost: organic matter that has undergone progressive decomposition by microbial and macrobial activity until it is reduced to a spongy, fluffy texture. Added to soil of any type, it improves the soil's ability to hold air and water and to drain well.

Corm: the swollen energy-storing structure, analogous to a bulb, under the soil at the base of the stem of plants such as crocus and gladiolus.

Crown: the base of a plant at, or just beneath, the surface of the soil where the roots meet the stems.

Cultivar: a CULTIvated VARiety. It is a naturally occurring form of a plant that has been identified as special or superior and is purposely selected for propagation and production.

Deadhead: a pruning technique that removes faded flower heads from plants to improve their appearances, abort seed production, and stimulate further flowering.

Deciduous plants: unlike evergreens, these trees and shrubs lose their leaves in the fall.

Desiccation: drying out of foliage tissues, usually due to drought or wind.

Division: the practice of splitting apart perennial plants to create several smaller-rooted segments. The practice is useful for controlling the plant's size and for acquiring more plants; it is also essential to the health and continued flowering of certain ones.

Dormancy: the period, usually the winter, when perennial plants temporarily cease active growth and rest. Dormant is the verb form, as used in this sentence: *Some plants, like spring-blooming bulbs, go dormant in the summer.*

Established: the point at which a newly planted tree, shrub, or flower begins to produce new growth, either foliage or stems. This is an indication that the roots have recovered from transplant shock and have begun to grow and spread.

Evergreen: perennial plants that do not lose their foliage annually with the onset of winter. Needled or broadleaf foliage will persist and continues to function on a plant through one or more winters, aging and dropping unobtrusively in cycles of three or four years or more.

Floret: a tiny flower, usually one of many forming a cluster, that comprises a single blossom.

Foliar: of or about foliage—usually refers to the practice of spraying foliage, as in fertilizing or treating with insecticide; leaf tissues absorb liquid directly for fast results, and the soil is not affected.

Germinate: to sprout. Germination is a fertile seed's first stage of development.

Graft (union): the point on the stem of a woody plant with sturdier roots where a stem from a highly ornamental plant is inserted so that it will join with it. Roses are commonly grafted.

Hands: the female flowers on a banana tree; they turn into bananas.

Hardscape: the permanent, structural, nonplant part of a landscape, such as walls, sheds, pools, patios, arbors, and walkways.

Herbaceous: plants having fleshy or soft stems that die back with frost; the opposite of woody.

Hybrid: a plant that is the result of intentional or natural cross-pollination between two or more plants of the same species or genus.

Low water demand: describes plants that tolerate dry soil for varying periods of time. Typically, they have succulent, hairy, or silvery-gray foliage and tuberous roots or taproots.

Mulch: a layer of material over bare soil to protect it from erosion and compaction by rain, and to discourage weeds. It may be inorganic (gravel, fabric) or organic (wood chips, bark, pine needles, chopped leaves).

Naturalize: (*a*) to plant seeds, bulbs, or plants in a random, informal pattern as they would appear in their natural habitats; (*b*) to adapt to and spread throughout adopted habitats (a tendency of some nonnative plants).

Nectar: the sweet fluid produced by glands on flowers that attract pollinators such as hummingbirds and honeybees, for whom it is a source of energy.

Organic material, organic matter: any material or debris that is derived from plants. It is carbon-based material capable of undergoing decomposition and decay.

Peat moss: organic matter from peat sedges (United States) or sphagnum mosses (Canada), often used to improve soil texture. The acidity of sphagnum peat moss makes it ideal for boosting or maintaining soil acidity while also improving its drainage.

Perennial: a flowering plant that lives over two or more seasons. Many die back with frost, but their roots survive the winter and generate new shoots in the spring.

pH: a measurement of the relative acidity (low pH) or alkalinity (high pH) of soil or water based on a scale of 1 to 14, 7 being neutral. Individual plants require soil to be within a certain range so that nutrients can dissolve in moisture and be available to them.

Pinch: to remove tender stems and/or leaves by pressing them between thumb and forefinger. This pruning technique encourages branching, compactness, and flowering in plants, or it removes aphids clustered at growing tips.

Pollen: the yellow, powdery grains in the center of a flower. A plant's male sex cells, they are transferred to the female plant parts by means of wind or animal pollinators to fertilize them and create seeds.

Raceme: an arrangement of single-stalked flowers along an elongated, unbranched axis.

Rhizome: a swollen energy-storing stem structure, similar to a bulb, that lies horizontally in the soil, with roots emerging from its lower surface and growth shoots from a growing point at or near its tip, as in bearded iris.

Rootbound (or potbound): the condition of a plant that has been confined in a container too long, its roots having been forced to wrap around themselves and even swell out of the container. Successful transplanting or repotting requires untangling and trimming away of some of the matted roots.

Root flare: the transition at the base of a tree trunk where the bark tissue begins to differentiate and roots begin to form just before entering the soil. This area should not be covered with soil when planting a tree.

Self-seeding: the tendency of some plants to sow their seeds freely around the yard. It creates many seedlings the following season that may or may not be welcome.

Semievergreen: tending to be evergreen in a mild climate but deciduous in a rigorous one.

Shearing: the pruning technique whereby plant stems and branches are cut uniformly with long-bladed pruning shears (hedge shears) or powered hedge trimmers. It is used when creating and maintaining hedges and topiary.

Slow-acting fertilizer: fertilizer that is water insoluble and therefore releases its nutrients gradually as a function of soil temperature, moisture, and related microbial activity. Typically granular, it may be organic or synthetic.

Succulent growth: the sometimes undesirable production of fleshy, water-storing leaves or stems that results from overfertilization.

Sucker: a new-growing shoot. Underground plant roots produce suckers to form new stems and spread by means of these suckering roots to form large plantings, or colonies. Some plants produce root suckers or branch suckers as a result of pruning or wounding.

Tuber: a type of underground storage structure in a plant stem, analogous to a bulb. It generates roots below and stems above ground (example: dahlia).

Variegated: having various colors or color patterns. The term usually refers to plant foliage that is streaked, edged, blotched, or mottled with a contrasting color—often green with yellow, cream, or white.

White grubs: fat, off-white, wormlike larvae of Japanese beetles. They reside in the soil and feed on plant (especially grass) roots until summer when they emerge as beetles to feed on plant foliage.

Wings: (*a*) the corky tissue that forms edges along the twigs of some woody plants such as winged euonymus; (*b*) the flat, dried extension of tissue on some seeds, such as maple, that catch the wind and help them disseminate.

Bibliography

Reference Books

Armitage, Allan M. *Herbaceous Perennial Plants.* Champaign, Illinois: Stipes Publishing, 1997.

Bender, Steve, editor. *The Southern Living Garden Problem Solver.* Birmingham, Alabama: Oxmoor House, 1999.

Darke, Rick. *Color Encyclopedia of Ornamental Grasses.* Portland, Oregon: Timber Press, 1999.

Dirr, Michael A. *Manual of Woody Landscape Plants.* Champaign, Illinois: Stipes Publishing, 1998.

DiSabito-Aust, Tracy. *The Well-Tended Perennial Garden.* Portland, Oregon: Timber Press, 1998.

Heriteau, Jacqueline and Marc Cathey, editors. *The National Arboretum Book of Outstanding Garden Plants.* New York, New York: Simon & Schuster, 1990.

Hoshizaki, Barbara Joe and Robbin C. Moran. *Fern Grower's Manual.* Portland, Oregon: Timber Press, 2001.

General Reading

Bender, Steve and Felder Rushing. *Passalong Plants.* Chapel Hill, North Carolina: The University of North Carolina Press, 1993.

Hodgson, Larry. *Perennials for Every Purpose.* Emmaus, Pennsylvania: Rodale Press, 2000.

Holmes, Roger, editor. *Taylor's Guide to Ornamental Grasses.* Boston, Massachusetts: Houghton Mifflin Co., 1997.

Ogden, Scott. *Garden Bulbs for the South.* Dallas, Texas: Taylor Publishing, 1994.

Roth, Susan A. *The Four-Season Landscape.* Emmaus, Pennsylvania: Rodale Press, 1994.

Sedenko, Jerry. *The Butterfly Garden.* New York, New York: Villard Books, 1991.

Xerces Society, The, and The Smithsonian Institution. *Butterfly Gardening.* San Francisco, California: Sierra Club Books, 1998.

Photography Credits

Thomas Eltzroth: pages 9, 16, 28, 32, 34, 36, 42, 44, 54, 56, 58, 60, 62, 66, 68, 74, 76, 78, 80, 82, 86, 94, 96
Jerry Pavia: pages 10, 11, 14, 18, 26, 46, 50, 84, 90, 100, 102, 106, 110
Liz Ball and Rick Ray: pages 24, 40, 52, 72, 92, 98, 104, 108
Pam Harper: pages 30, 38, 64, 70, 88
Felder Rushing: pages 8, 20
Lorenzo Gunn: page 12
Ralph Snodsmith: page 48
Andre Viette: page 22

Plant Index

126

Want to know more about Tennessee gardening?

Interested in terrific trees for Tennessee? Do you want healthful and tasty herbs, fruits, and vegetables from your Tennessee garden? How about fantastic Tennessee flowers?

If you enjoy *50 Great Shrubs for Tennessee*, you will appreciate similar books featuring Tennessee trees, vegetables (including fruits and herbs), and flowers. These valuable books also deserve a place in your gardening library.

50 Great Trees for Tennessee

Author Judy Lowe recommends fifty great trees for Tennessee. She offers fantastic options on small flowering trees, great evergreens, and trees that delight with multiseason interest.

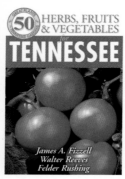

50 Great Herbs, Fruits and Vegetables for Tennessee

If you are inclined to "edibles" in your Tennessee garden, this is the book for you. It provides valuable advice on how to select, plant, and grow tasty herbs, luscious fruits, and flavorful vegetables. Written by James A. Fizzell, Walter Reeves, and Felder Rushing, this book offers more than seventy-five years of gardening wisdom all in an easy-to-use format.

50 Great Flowers for Tennessee

Judy Lowe shares her personal recommendations on fifty delightful flowering plants for Tennessee. From colorful annuals that give you spring-to-fall color, to hard-working perennials that return year after year, you will find much to choose from in this book.

Look for each of these books today.

50 GREAT SHRUBS *for* TENNESSEE

Do you want straightforward and reliable advice to help you decide which shrubs to plant in your Tennessee garden? Now Judy Lowe shares her wisdom and practical advice to help you beautify your home with the landscape of your dreams!

50 Great Shrubs for Tennessee features:

- ○ Judy's recommendations on the top-performing shrubs for Tennessee
- ○ How to plant, water, fertilize, and control pests
- ○ How to get top performance from every shrub
- ○ Easy Tips offer inside information you can use *now*
- ○ Valuable landscape design tips

50 Great Shrubs for Tennessee will become your valued friend as you plan, beautify, and enjoy your Tennessee garden.

Judy Lowe is the former Garden Editor of the *Chattanooga Times-Free Press*. With more than twenty years' experience, Judy has shared her gardening wisdom with thousands of readers. Also she has contributed articles to *Women's Day* and *Southern Living* magazines. She is currently Garden Editor at *The Christian Science Monitor*.

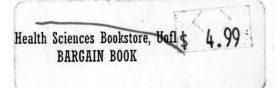

$12.99 U.S.
ISBN 1-591860-78-4

COOL
SPRINGS
PRESS
A Division of Thomas Nelson, Inc.
www.ThomasNelson.com

51299
9 781591 860785